The Nicene Creed is an immensely important text for the life of the church and yet it is a creed that many know little about. What is the Nicene Creed? Is it biblical? And does it continue to be relevant for us today? These are the very questions Dr. David Robinson addresses in this fine study. In *A Pattern of Sound Words*, one will find an engaging and accessible guide for understanding the Nicene Creed. Through extensive engagement with biblical texts and historical theological sources, Robinson shows the Nicene Creed's alignment with the teachings of Scripture and the historic witness of the church. He therefore displays that this Creed continues to be deeply relevant for Christians today.

Jonathan N. Cleland, Ph.D.
Adjunct Professor at Heritage College and Seminary,
Cambridge, Ontario, Canada

Creeds and confessions anchor Christians in foundational truth amid the restless tides of uncertainty. Aware of this need, Robinson turns his historical and theological lens upon the Nicene Creed, magnifying its depth and enduring relevance. Through his careful study, readers gain a clearer vision of this ancient confession as a timeless, biblical compass for faith and fidelity—one capable of steadying the soul through every spiritual storm.

Coleman M. Ford, Ph.D.
Assistant Professor of Humanities and
Chair of the Department of Humanities at
Texas Baptist College, Forth Worth, TX

On the 1700th anniversary of the Nicene Creed, Pastor David Robinson provides a very accessible volume detailing the historic realities occurring in the 4th century and earlier that precipitated the need for a creedal statement. He ably guides the reader on the Creed's critical explanation of the Godhead, Christ, and the Trinity at a time when the Arian heresy was beginning to be prevalent.

Our own Fellowship of Churches completed a thorough revision of our Affirmation of Faith in late 2025 and often referred to and appreciated the Nicene Creed among other historic creeds and confessions. Our motivation to revise was to prepare our churches for the 21st century. I can only imagine the Church Fathers were similarly motivated to prepare a creed that would ensure orthodoxy among Christ's church for centuries to come.

My thanks to David for focusing our attention on what we 'believe and confess' as essential and helping to make a 1700-year-old creedal statement accessible to a new generation.

Rev. Steven Jones
National President, The Fellowship of Evangelical Baptist Churches in Canada

DAVID C. ROBINSON

A Pattern *of* Sound Words

A GUIDE TO THE NICENE CREED

A Pattern of Sound Words: A Guide to the Nicene Creed
by David C. Robinson

© 2025 by David C. Robinson

Heritage Seminary Press
Heritage College and Seminary
175 Holiday Inn Drive
Cambridge, ON
Canada
N3C 3T2

All rights reserved. This book or any portion thereof may not be reproduced or used in any manner whatsoever without the express written permission of the publisher except for the use of brief quotations in a book review.

Unless otherwise noted, Scripture quotations are from The ESV® Bible (The Holy Bible, English Standard Version®), copyright © 2001 by Crossway, a publishing ministry of Good News Publishers. Used by permission. All rights reserved.

Cover design and layout by Dustin Benge

978-1-77484-185-3 (eBook)
978-1-77484-184-6 (paperback)

Contents

	Foreword	*7*
	Introduction	*9*
1	We Believe in God the Father	*19*
2	We Believe in God the Son	*31*
3	For Us Men and for Our Salvation	*43*
4	We Believe in the Holy Spirit	*71*
	Coda	*95*

Foreword

In his masterful study of the unfolding of early Christian thought, historian Jaroslav Pelikan once noted that the "climax of the doctrinal development of the early church was the dogma of the Trinity."[1] And the textual expression of that climax is undoubtedly the Niceno-Constantinopolitan Creed, more popularly known as the Nicene Creed, which was issued at the Council of Constantinople (381), in which Jesus Christ is unequivocally declared to be "true God" and "of one being (*homoousios*) with the Father" and the Holy Spirit is said to be the "Lord and Giver of life," who "together with the Father and the Son is worshipped and glorified." The original Nicene Creed, issued by the Council of Nicaea in 325, had made a similar statement about the Son and his deity, but nothing had been said about the Holy Spirit beyond the statement "[We believe] in the Holy Spirit." When the deity of the Spirit was subsequently questioned in the 360s and 370s, it was necessary to expand the Nicene Creed to include a statement about the deity of the Holy Spirit. In the end, this expansion involved

---

1 Jaroslav Pelikan, *The Christian Tradition: Vol. 1: The Emergence of the Catholic Tradition (100-600)* (Chicago; London: The University of Chicago Press, 1971), 172.

the drafting of the creedal statement issued by the Council of Constantinople.

But what do these ancient battles over the nature of God and the persons of Jesus Christ and his Holy Spirit have to do with us in our day? There are some Bible-believing Christians who would quickly answer this question with an adamant reply: "Nothing. We have no need of man-made creeds and confessions. All we need is the Bible." To be sure, the Bible is the standard by which all other Christian texts must be measured. But it is the height of folly to ignore what God the Holy Spirit has given us in the history of the Church: the lives of God's saints and their writings—sermons and prayers, hymns and diaries, and creeds and confessions. The Nicene Creed, as Dr. Robinson powerfully shows us in this fresh study of this ancient text, is deeply relevant to the modern day and has rich wisdom for our common life in Christ. The Nicene Creed is immensely valuable since it sums up in a short compass the entire biblical witness about the nature of the true and living God. He is the Father and the Son and the Holy Spirit, unto whom be glory and honour forever and ever.

Michael A. G. Azad Haykin
Dundas, Ontario
May 28, 2025

Introduction

We believe. This short sentence captures a truth basic to humanity. We all believe. No one can honestly claim, "I do not believe." Everyone believes and everyone believes something. How can we avoid the question: "Is what I believe true?"

The Nicene Creed begins with this phrase, "We believe." What follows this opening statement is a summary statement of the truth which Christians believe. The final form of the Creed was written at the Council of Constantinople in 381. It is a confession of faith which is the fruit of three centuries of the Church's worship of the Triune God revealed in Scripture.

Some of the words and phrases sound strange to us. Why do we confess that the Son is "eternally begotten" or that he is "true God from true God"? Why do we confess that the Church is "one, holy, catholic, and apostolic"? What do the words "catholic" and "apostolic" mean? In this short book, I want to consider the meaning and significance of each word and phrase in the Nicene Creed, in order to uncover and present its rich theological and biblical doctrine.

My hope is that the truth expressed in these words and phrases will commend itself to contemporary Christians. Before I turn our attention to the Nicene Creed, it is important to situate the Creed in its historical context and it is helpful to address the question of why we should have creeds in the first place and why we should confess the Nicene Creed in particular.

Why Creeds?

First, why creeds? I would answer, simply, because "we believe." Faith is universal. Everyone believes. As I asked at the outset, the question is, "what do you believe and is it true?" Christians believe the truth of the Gospel, the Good News of Jesus Christ. The Apostle Paul writes in Romans 10:9-10: "if you confess with your mouth that Jesus is Lord and believe in your heart that God raised him from the dead, you will be saved. For with the heart one believes and is justified, and with the mouth one confesses and is saved."[1]

Notice the relationship between the two verbs Paul uses, confess and believe. It is a relationship of heart and mouth, what we believe in our hearts we confess with our mouths. We believe in our hearts that God raised Jesus from the dead; we confess with our mouths that Jesus is Lord.

Confession is personal and public: *we* believe and *we* confess. The Greek word translated "confess" is *homologeō*, which literally means to speak the same words: *homo* (same) + *logos* (word). Our confession is a public expression of shared belief; we confess one and the same faith with one and the same voice. Our confession is not a matter of personal opinion or belief – *we* believe. It's not simply *my* faith, but *our* faith, and it's "the faith that was once for all delivered to the saints" (Jude 1:3). It's the "good deposit" that Paul entrusted to Timothy and commanded Timothy to guard and entrust to faithful men, who will be able to teach others (2 Tim 1:14; 2:1-2). It's our faith, yes, but it's our faith that we receive and guard and pass on.

---

1 Quotations from Scripture are from the *English Standard Version* (Crossway, 2016).

Introduction

The Nicene Creed: The Portrait of the King

The Nicene Creed is a confession of faith in the Triune God, who is revealed and made known to us in Scripture. But why do we need it or any other confession of faith when we have God's inspired and inerrant Word? Can (or should) we not simply confess, "Jesus is Lord" as Paul says in Romans 10:9? Does the use of creeds and confessions undermine the sufficiency and authority of Scripture?

Irenaeus of Lyons considered these questions in the second century. At the time, there were Gnostic Christians who confessed, "Jesus is Lord" (Rom 10:9), but what they meant by that confession denied what Scripture affirmed. They denied that the Lord Jesus was incarnate, that he suffered and died in our place for our sin, and that he was raised in the flesh on the third day. They said they believed in the resurrection, but for them resurrection meant spiritual enlightenment and liberation from the body.

Both true believers and Gnostics were confessing the lordship of Christ and his resurrection, but the Gnostics denied what Scripture affirmed about the lordship of Christ and his resurrection. In response to the Gnostics, the Church had a confession of faith that affirmed what Scripture revealed and taught about God. Irenaeus reminds his readers of this confession in his book against the Gnostics:

> The church, dispersed throughout the world to the ends of the earth, received from the apostles and their disciples the faith in one God the Father Almighty, who made heaven and earth and sea and all that is in them, and in one Christ Jesus, the Son of God, incarnate for our salvation, and in the Holy Spirit, who through the prophets predicted the dispensations of God: the advent, the birth from the Virgin, the passion, the resurrection from the dead, and the ascension of the beloved Jesus Christ our Lord in the flesh into the heavens, and his coming from

the heavens in the glory of the Father to recapitulate all things and raise up all flesh of the human race. (*Against Heresies* I.10.1)[2]

This confession is simply a summary of what the Bible declares about the Triune God, creation, and redemption.

In the second century, Christians called this confession "the rule of faith." The rule of faith functions like a ruler. We use a ruler to measure and draw straight lines. Likewise, various ideas, truth claims, and interpretations of Scripture can be measured by the rule of faith and can be proven straight (or crooked) by their alignment with the rule of faith.

The rule of faith helped Christians recognize false teaching. Irenaeus writes that the Gnostics tried to prove their doctrine by "changing the interpretations and twisting the exegesis" of Scripture (*Against Heresies* I.3.6).[3] He uses an analogy to illustrate this twisted exegesis. He compares Scripture to a mosaic portrait of a king. Looking at isolated passages of Scripture is like looking at individual stones or tiles in a mosaic. When you step back, you see that there is a logic and an order to the stones that together presents the portrait of the king. The rule of faith (or creed) is analogous to the image of the king. It's the picture we see when we look at the Bible as a whole.

The Gnostics had taken the various stones of the mosaic and rearranged them, producing the image of a dog or a fox. They quoted the Bible, but they twisted it to present their own false doctrine. Irenaeus warns that false teachers "contradict the order and the continuity of the Scriptures" (*Against Heresies* I.8.1).[4] There's an order and continuity in the Scriptures, which provides the basic structure and content of biblical doctrine. Creeds present this basic outline of biblical doctrine. They provide a "pattern of sounds words" (2 Tim 1:13).

---

2   *Irenaeus of Lyons*, trans. Robert Grant (New York: Routledge, 1997), 70–71.
3   *Irenaeus of Lyons*, trans. Grant, 47.
4   *Irenaeus of Lyons*, trans. Grant, 50.

The Nicene Creed is a fourth-century version of the rule of faith, which provides the basic outline of God's self-revelation in Scripture. It is the portrait of the king. If someone uses Scripture to present a different portrait, we will know it's false.

Creeds and confessions do not undermine the sufficiency, inerrancy, and authority of God's Word. On the contrary, they acknowledge and affirm God's Word. The Nicene Creed follows the order and continuity of the Scriptures and gives us the basic structure and content of biblical doctrine.

The Council of Nicaea, 325

The Nicene Creed did not fall out of the sky one day in the 4th century. It's important to situate the Creed in its historical context. We call it the Nicene Creed because it was initially composed at the Council of Nicaea in 325. The Roman Emperor Constantine had called the council to address divisions within the Church. Bishops from various parts of the Roman empire travelled to Nicaea for the council. Many of them had been tortured for their faith before Constantine ended persecution. Some were beaten and scourged, some had their eyes gouged out and their noses split or cut off. And, yet, here they were, hobbled, maimed, and gathered in an imperial palace, at the emperor's request and at the emperor's expense.

They debated and discussed a variety of doctrinal and practical concerns, such as the date of Easter; however, the primary source of controversy and division was the teaching of a priest in Alexandria named Arius. Arius had a narrow doctrine of God. In his view, one of the defining attributes of God is that he is unbegotten. For Arius, "unbegottenness" was definitive of divinity.

Arius had philosophical and theological reasons for this position, but his primary concern was that to maintain a crystal-clear distinction and separation between the Creator and creation. Pagan theology too often conflated divinity and humanity. In the pagan myths, the gods were always getting mixed up and compromised with human beings. Arius wanted to recognize and defend God's absolute transcendence. There was a lot of begetting among the pagan gods, but the one true God is unbegotten.

We can appreciate Arius's desire to maintain a clear distinction between the Creator and the creation; however, his insistence that "unbegottenness" is definitive of divinity did not square with God's own self-revelation in Scripture. God's Word declares that the Son of God is God (John 1:1) and is begotten from the Father (John 1:14; 1:18; 3:16; 3:18). For Arius, the Son cannot be God because he is begotten and God must be unbegotten. Thus, Arius taught that the Son is a creature and not God.

His teaching was popular. It's reported that the dockworkers in Alexandria used to sing this little ditty about the Son: "There once was a time when he was not." When the bishops gathered in Nicaea, the primary item on the agenda was to examine and respond to Arius's teaching. Against Arius, the Nicene Creed confesses what Scripture reveals: "We believe in one Lord, Jesus Christ, the only-begotten Son of God, eternally begotten from the Father, Light from Light, true God from true God, begotten, not made, of the same being as the Father."[5]

While the Creed's confession concerning the Son directly opposes Arianism, we should also note its first line concerning the Father. The Creed does not begin, "We believe in One God, the Unbegotten," but "We believe in One God, the Father." We confess that the one God is Father, not unbegotten, but Father. And if the one God is Father, he is also Son. Through the Son we know the Father, not the Unbegotten.

From Nicaea to Constantinople, 381

The Council of Nicaea is not the end of the story of Arianism, nor is it the end of the story of the Nicene Creed. In fact, the Council of Nicaea concludes the opening scene of a dramatic theological conflict that would last for decades and would not be resolved until the Council

---

5 *Creeds & Confessions of Faith in the Christian Tradition*, vol 1, eds. Jaroslav Pelikan and Valerie Hotchkiss (New Haven: Yale University Press, 2003), 163 (translation modified).

of Constantinople in 381. What we call the Nicene Creed is actually the creed of this later council in Constantinople, which revised and supplemented the creed of Nicaea.

The historical record of what happened between 325 and 381 includes some of the most intriguing and harrowing events in church history and involves some the greatest personalities in church history. The story of these tumultuous decades in the fourth century is the story of conflict and controversy between emperors, bishops, monks, and councils. Various creeds where composed and commended and few people at the time thought the creed of Nicaea would become the universal test of orthodoxy.

Here is the creed of Nicaea:

> We believe in one God, the Father Almighty, Maker of all things visible and invisible.
>
> And in one Lord Jesus Christ the Son of God, the Only-begotten of the Father, that is from the being of the Father, God of God, Light of Light, true God of true God, begotten not made, the same being (*homoousion*) with the Father, through whom all things came to be, both those in heaven and those in earth; for us men and for our salvation he came down and became incarnate, became man, suffered and rose again on the third day, and ascended into the heavens, and is coming to judge the living and the dead.
>
> And in the Holy Spirit.[6]

The word *homoousios* ("the same being") was the central point of contention. Some argued the term should be dropped or softened to *homoiousios* ("similar of like being"). The Arians argued for terms like *heteroousios* ("different being") or *anhomoios* ("not the same").

---

6 *Creeds & Confessions of Faith in the Christian Tradition*, eds. Jaroslav Pelikan and Valerie Hotchkiss, 157, 158 (translation modified).

Some historians view the whole controversy as a primary example of religion's corruptive influence in society. The Roman Empire was being fractured by squabbling over vowels. But vowels matter, like whether a person runs or ruins a company.

In the decades following the Council of Nicaea, those who defended the Nicene confession that the Son is *homoousios* with the Father were in the minority. In the face of Arian bishops and emperors, Athanasius of Alexandria (ca.296/98–373) preached and wrote in defense of *homoousios* and the full divinity of the Son, earning him the epithet *contra mundum* – against the world.[7]

He was not alone. Bishops and theologians like Basil of Caesarea (330–379), Gregory of Nyssa (ca.335–394), and Gregory of Nazianzus (329–390) systematically deconstructed Arian theology and constructed an orthodox bulwark in defense of the divinity of the Son.[8] Even so, there was no guarantee the theological writings of a few bishops would overturn decades of Arian dominance. When Gregory of Nazianzus was appointed to serve as the bishop of the Nicene Church in the imperial capital of Constantinople, he describes the small Nicene remnant as "a slight trace and relic of a flock, without order or shepherds or bounds, with neither right to pasture nor the defense of a fold" (*Or*. 42.2).[9] The church gathered in his cousin's villa. He named it "Anastasia." Constantinople was an Arian stronghold. If Nicene orthodoxy had any hope, it needed resurrection.

Gregory began preaching on the Trinity. Five of these sermons stand out: the *Five Theological Orations* (*Orations* 27–31), which he delivered in the late summer of 380. *Orations* 29 and 30 consider the relationship of the Father and the Son and defend the full divinity of

---

7   Athanasius, *On the Incarnation*, trans. John Behr, Popular Patristics Series 44B (New York: SVS Press, 2011); *Works of the Spirit: Athanasius the Great and Didymus the Blind*, trans. Mark DelCogliano, Andrew Radde-Gallwitz, and Lewis Ayres, Popular Patristics Series 43 (New York: SVS Press, 2011).

8   Basil the Great, *On the Holy Spirit*, trans. David Anderson (Crestwood, NY: SVS Press, 1980); Gregory of Nazianzus, *On God and Christ: The Five Theological Orations and Two Letters to Cledonius*, trans. Frederick Williams and Lionel R. Wickham (Crestwood, NY: SVS Press, 2002).

9   Translated by John Behr in *The Nicene Faith* (Crestwood, NY: SVS Press, 2004), 327.

Introduction

the Son. *Oration* 31 considers the person and work of the Holy Spirit and defends the full divinity of the Spirit. The creed of Nicaea presents no doctrine of the Holy Spirit. It simply affirmed, "We believe in the Holy Spirit." Just as the divinity of Son needed to be exegetically defended and explained, so the divinity of the Spirit needed to be exegetically defended and explained. Athanasius had written a defense of the Spirit's divinity in the 360s.[10] In the 370s, Basil of Caesarea and Gregory of Nazianzus affirmed and developed Athanasius's initial orthodox defence and articulation of the doctrine of God the Holy Spirit.[11]

In the year 380, the same year Gregory was preaching the orthodox doctrine of the Trinity in the small Church of the Resurrection, a new emperor ascended the imperial throne. Theodosius affirmed Nicene orthodoxy. He wanted to bring an end to the Arian controversy once for all and unify the Church around a common orthodox confession.

Theodosius called a council of bishops which met in Constantinople in 381. The crucible of theological controversy in the middle decades of the fourth century forged a robust and refined trinitarian doctrine, which was finally and formally summarized in the revised and amended creed of the Council of Constantinople. Against the Arians, the Creed affirmed the doctrinal convictions of the earlier Council in Nicaea concerning the divinity of the Son. The Council also added a third paragraph, confessing Christian faith in the Holy Spirit and what we believe about the Church. Although the final form and content of the Creed was set at the Council of Constantinople, it was seen as a clarification and confirmation of the earlier creed of Nicaea, which is why we still call it the Nicene Creed.

---

10 Athanasius, "Letters to Serapion on the Holy Spirit" in *Works on the Spirit*.
11 Basil of Caesarea, *On the Holy Spirit*; and Gregory of Nazianzus, "Oration 31" in *On God and Christ*.

Here is the Nicene Creed:

> We believe in one God, the Father, the Almighty, Maker of heaven and earth, of all things visible and invisible.
>
> We believe in one Lord, Jesus Christ, the only-begotten Son of God, eternally begotten from the Father, Light from Light, true God from true God, begotten not made, the same being with the Father, through whom all things were made. For us men and for our salvation he came down from heaven; he was incarnate by the Holy Spirit and the Virgin Mary, and became man. He was crucified for us under Pontius Pilate; he suffered and was buried. On the third day he rose again according to the Scriptures; he ascended into heaven and is seated at the right hand of the Father. He will come again in glory to judge the living and the dead, and his kingdom will have no end.
>
> We believe in the Holy Spirit, the Lord, the Giver of Life, who proceeds from the Father [and the Son]. With the Father and the Son he is worshipped and glorified. He has spoken through the Prophets. We believe in one, holy, catholic, and apostolic Church. We confess one baptism for the forgiveness of sins. And we look for the resurrection of the dead and the life of the world to come. Amen.[12]

---

12 *Creeds & Confessions of Faith in the Christian Tradition*, eds. Jaroslav Pelikan and Valerie Hotchkiss, 163 (translation modified).

1
We Believe in God the Father

We believe in one God, the Father, the Almighty, Maker of heaven and earth, of all things visible and invisible.

We Believe in One God

The Nicene Creed begins with a confession of monotheism: "We believe in one God." This confession grounds the Creed in biblical revelation and the confession of Israel: "Hear, O Israel: The Lord our God, the Lord is one" (Deut 6:4). Israel's confession is a revelation from God himself. He speaks and calls Israel to listen.

God's revelation to Israel is a redemptive rebuke to the polytheism of the ancient world. Throughout biblical history, the surrounding nations of the Ancient Near East and the later Greco-Roman world were subject to polytheism. People lived their day-to-day lives caught in the fray of warring deities. Religion amounted to a tenuous set of negotiations and transactions with a pantheon of capricious and petty gods. The prophets of Baal give us a sense of what pagan worship looked like: calling, limping, crying, cutting, and raving (1 Kings 18:20-40).

In the midst of such religious chaos, the one true God called

Abraham and made a covenant with him. He said to Abraham and his descendants, "I am yours and you are mine" (Ex 6:7). Israel does not only confess "The Lord is one" but "The Lord *our* God, the Lord is one." The one God is *our* God. Canaanites could never say *our* Baal. God condescends and identifies with his people. The one God is the God of Abraham, Isaac, and Jacob.

The Lord is one and he alone is God. As he declares through the prophet,

> "I am the Lord, and there is no other,
> besides me there is no God." (Is 45:5)

The Apostle Paul repeats this prophetic declaration to the nations, "we know that an idol has no real existence, and that there is no God but one. For although there may be so-called gods in heaven or on earth – as indeed there are many 'gods' and many 'lords' – yet for us there is one God." (1 Cor 8:4-6a)

The revelation and confession that God is one was an announcement of salvation to the nations living under the darkness and tyranny of polytheism. Day-to-day life is not caught up in the conflict of capricious deities. Our lives are in the hands of the Creator of heaven and earth, who is also the Redeemer, who calls to the nations,

> "Turn to me and be saved,
> all the ends of the earth!
> For I am God, and there is no other." (Is 45:22)

While the pagan temples of the ancient world have not been rebuilt, the tyranny of polytheism has been revived. People are once again navigating life in submission to various competing ideologies and worldviews.

In the midst of such fragmented loyalties, the Church continues to confess, "we believe in one God" and flowing from this confession, we declare with the Apostle, "There is one body and one Spirit – just as you were called to the one hope that belongs to your call – one Lord, one faith, one baptism, one God and Father of all, who is over all and through all and in all" (Ephesians 4:4-5). Yes, we believe in one God – who is over all and through all and in all – and whenever we confess that God is one, we also confess that there is one Spirit, one Lord, and one Father. The one God is Triune.

Gregory of Nazianzus, a pastor and theologian in the fourth century, can help us understand our faith in the Triune God. To begin, Gregory warns that we cannot say more about the Triune God than Scripture reveals:

> For me it is enough to hear that there is a Son, and that he is from the Father, and that the one is Father and the other is Son. I do not trouble myself beyond this, lest I become just like those voices that go completely hoarse from shouting too loudly, or the eye that strains towards the rays of the sun. (*Oration* 20.10)[1]

Looking to Scripture, Gregory notes that the names Father, Son, and Spirit are tied to their relationship with one another and the manner in which the Son and the Spirit have their being from the Father.

The Son and Spirit are what the Father is, because they are from the Father. The unity and oneness of God has its source in the Father's being, which he shares with the Son and the Spirit. Scripture reveals that the Son is "the only-begotten from the Father" (John 1:14) and the Spirit "proceeds from the Father" (John 15:26). The Son is the Son because he is begotten from the Father. The Father is the Father because he has begotten the Son. The Spirit is the Spirit because he proceeds from the Father.

The Father is unbegotten, the Son is begotten, and the Spirit proceeds. The terms "unbegotten," "begotten," and "procession" are not definitive of God's divine being; rather, they signify three properties,

---

1 *Gregory of Nazianzus*, trans. Brian Daley (London: Routledge, 2007), 103-104.

which distinguish the three persons and their relationship to one another as Father, Son, and Spirit. The one God has revealed himself in Scripture as Father, Son, and Spirit. Given this divine revelation, Gregory writes, "The aim is to safeguard the distinctness of the three [persons] within the single nature and quality of the Godhead ... The three are one in their Godhead and the one is three in properties" (*Oration* 31.9).[2]

Whenever we are reading Scripture, praying, singing, contemplating God, we must be careful to safeguard the unity and oneness of God and the distinction of the three persons. The Father, Son, and Spirit are one God and the one God is Father, Son, and Spirit. When we are thinking about the Triune God, we must remember that God is eternal. To say that the Son and Spirit have their being *from* the Father does not mean they have their being *after* the Father. The Father has always been the Father; the Son has always been the Son; and the Spirit has always been the Spirit.[3]

Gregory also warns against analogies for the Trinity: "There is one God, one supreme nature, where can I find analogy to show you? Are you looking for one from your environment here in this world?" (*Oration* 31.10)[4] Analogies for the Trinity will only reduce and obscure our understanding. We cannot look to the world around us to understand the Son's generation and the Spirit's procession.

Even so, the Bible says that the Son is begotten from the Father (John 1:14) and the Spirit proceeds from the Father (John 15:26). What does this mean? How should we understand the Son's generation and the Spirit's procession? Gregory asks, "How, then, was [the Son] begotten?" And answers:

> God's begetting ought to have the tribute of our reverent silence. The important point is for you to learn that [the

---

2   *On God and Christ*, trans. Wickham, 123 (slightly modified).
3   Gregory of Nazianzus, *Oration* 29.2.
4   *On God and Christ*, trans. Wickham, 124.

Son] has been begotten. As to the way it happens, we shall not concede that even the angels, much less you, know that. Shall I tell you the way? It is a way known only to the begetting Father and the begotten Son. (*Oration* 29.8)[5]

Then Gregory asks, "What, then, is 'proceeding'?" and answers: "You explain the [unbegottennes] of the Father and I will give you a [physiological] account of the Son's begetting and the Spirit's proceeding – and let us go mad the pair of us for prying into God's secrets" (*Oration* 31:8).[6] Scripture reveals *that* the Son is begotten from the Father and the Spirit proceeds from the Father. Scripture does not explain *how* the Son is begotten and the Spirit proceeds. Such knowledge belongs to God and we dare not pry into such a divine mystery.

We should not conclude that there is nothing to be said about the identity and relationship of the Father, Son, and Spirit; however, when we confess our faith in the Triune God, we must be careful to avoid straying into heresy. Gregory shows us the straight path in one of his sermons:

> So we adore the Father and the Son and the Holy Spirit, distinguishing their personal properties but uniting their Godhead; and we neither blend the three into one thing, lest we be sick with Sabellius's disease, nor do we divide them into three alien and unrelated things, lest we share Arius's madness. Why should we act like those who try to straighten a plant bent over completely in one direction by forcibly training it the opposite way, correcting one deviation by another? Rather, we should straighten it midway between the two, and so take our position within the bounds of reverence. (*Oration* 20.5)[7]

---

5   *On God and Christ*, trans. Wickham, 76.
6   *On God and Christ*, trans. Wickham, 124.
7   *Gregory of Nazianzus*, trans. Daley, 100-101.

Gregory here positions orthodoxy between the opposite errors of Sabellianism and Arianism. Sebellius was concerned that speaking of three persons implied polytheism and so denied that there are three persons in the Godhead. This meant blending or confusing the Father, Son, and Spirit. This heresy is also known as modalism and is taught in Oneness Pentecostalism. Arianism denied the divinity of Son and the Spirit, making the Father, Son, and Spirit three alien and unrelated things. This heresy is taught by Jehovah's Witnesses.

Orthodoxy is a straight plant, neither bent to one side or the other: "we adore the Father and the Son and the Holy Spirit, distinguishing their personal properties but uniting their Godhead . . . and so we take our position within the bounds of reverence." Gregory was concerned that we have right belief. To believe rightly is to be orthodox, but orthodoxy cannot be reduced to right doctrine. Orthodoxy is right worship. Right theology rightly orients and defines our worship by placing us "within the bounds of reverence."

The Father, the Almighty

We believe in "God the Father, the Almighty." He is eternally the Father of the eternally begotten Son. When we confess our faith in God the Father, the Almighty, we confess our faith in the Father and the Son and the Spirit of the Father. Our confession of faith in God the Father is trinitarian, but is it also communicates something about salvation.

One of the central and most glorious truths of the Gospel is that we are made children of God and sons of God. Throughout John's Gospel, God the Son frequently refers to his Father, but after the resurrection, he commissions Mary in the garden: "go to my brothers and say to them, 'I am ascending to my Father and your Father, to my God and your God'" (John 20:17). God the Son reveals the Father and gives his life to redeem us from sin and death and judgment, so that we who believe in him are no longer "children of wrath" and "sons of disobedience" (Eph 2:2-3), but "dearly loved children" (Eph 5:1). The God and Father of our Lord Jesus Christ is our God and Father. Thus, the Apostle Paul declares, "For you did not receive the spirit of slavery to fall back into fear, but you have received the Spirit of adoption as sons, by whom we cry, 'Abba! Father!'" (Rom 8:15).

We confess that God our Father is the Almighty. I like how the Heidelberg Catechism elaborates this confession. In Question 26, the catechism asks:

> What do you believe when you say, "I believe in God, the Father almighty, creator of heaven and earth"?
>
> Answer: That the eternal Father of our Lord Jesus Christ, who out of nothing created heaven and earth and everything in them, who still upholds and rules them by his eternal counsel and providence, is my God and Father because of Christ the Son. I trust God so much that I do not doubt he will provide whatever I need for body and soul, and will turn to my good whatever adversity he sends upon me in this sad world. God is able to do this because he is almighty God and desires to do this because he is a faithful Father.[8]

Our secular society is in rebellion against God and this rebellion is manifest in a renunciation of fatherhood. Men renounce their calling and responsibility as fathers and the abandoned younger generation renounce their accountability to fathers.

Even so, our lived experience contradicts the pervasive and persistent rhetoric of liberation from patriarchy. Few people can deny the profound pain of fatherlessness. As God's dearly loved children, let us remember Hosea's prophetic prayer, "In you the fatherless find compassion" (Hosea 14:3) and let us pray with renewed zeal, "Our Father, who art in heaven, hallowed by thy name."

---

8 *The Heidelberg Catechism* (Grand Rapids, MI: Faith Alive Christian Resources), 18.

Maker of Heaven and Earth

God the Father, the Almighty, is "Maker of heaven and earth." This first line of the Nicene Creed confesses the fundamental distinction between the Creator and the creation. Idolatry confuses this Creator-creation distinction and worships the creation rather than the Creator. The fruit of such confusion is moral depravity and dehumanization: "Therefore God gave them up in the lusts of their hearts to impurity, to the dishonoring of their bodies among themselves, because they exchanged the truth about God for a lie and worshipped and served the creature rather than the Creator, who is blessed forever! Amen" (Rom 1:24-25).

A clear vision and convinced confession that God is the Maker of heaven and earth gives us clear moral vision and conviction. As the prophet Isaiah proclaims:

> Thus says God, the LORD,
>   who created the heavens and stretched them out,
>   who spread out the earth and what comes from it,
> who gives breath to the people on it
>   and spirit to those who walk in it:
> "I am the LORD; I have called you in righteousness;
>   I will take you by the hand and keep you" (Is 42:5-6a).

The Maker of heaven and earth has called us in righteousness. His world, his rules. When we submit to his rule, we know his providence. He has called us in righteousness and he will take us by the hand and keep us.

The Maker makes the rules and when we reject his rules and make our own rules, we are not only led in the way of moral depravity and dehumanization, we let go of his hand and lose the security of his keeping. If we refuse his way and walk our own path, we can expect anxiety and depression, and worse: "There is a way that seems right to a man, but its end is the way to death" (Prov 14:12).

Our Maker makes the rules. He has called us to walk according to his rules and he promises to take our hand and keep us in the way. Listen to how the Heidelberg Catechism explains God's providence:

> Question 27: What do you understand by the providence of God?
> Answer: Providence is the almighty and ever present power of God by which God upholds, as with his hand, heaven and earth and all creatures, and so rules them that leaf and blade, rain and drought, fruitful and lean years, food and drink, health and sickness, prosperity and poverty – all things, in fact, come to us not by chance but by his fatherly hand.
>
> Question 28: How does the knowledge of God's creation and providence help us?
> Answer: We can be patient when things go against us, thankful when things go well, and for the future we can have good confidence in our faithful God and Father that nothing in creation will separate us from his love. For all creatures are so completely in God's hand that without his will they can neither move nor be moved.[9]

The Maker of heaven and earth is the Father, the Almighty – and he is our Father.

> This is my Father's world:
> O let me ne'er forget
> That though the wrong seems oft so strong,
> God is the Ruler yet.
> This is my Father's world:
> Why should my heart be sad?

---

9 *The Heidelberg Catechism*, 19.

The Lord is King: let the heavens ring!
God reigns; let earth be glad![10]

All Things, Visible and Invisible

We confess in the Nicene Creed that God is the "Maker of heaven and earth, of all things, visible and invisible." His creation is both visible and invisible. It's helpful to distinguish what is invisible from what is unseen. The invention of microscopes and telescopes, ultrasound and x-ray machines, and CT and MRI scans, has allowed us to see what was hitherto unseen. Your femur bone and the rings of Saturn are not invisible. They are unseen. Technology has allowed us to see more and more of God's visible creation.

We must not conclude, however, that all that exists is what can be observed, or potentially observed. Technology has allowed greater observation, but God created all things, visible and invisible. His invisible creation cannot be observed by better technology, because it's not simply unseen, but invisible.

We confess that there is more to the world than meets the eye. We may categorize the invisible things as either intelligible or spiritual. There are intelligible aspects of God's creation. For example, there is an invisible order and coherence in what God has made, which is intelligible and beautiful, and when discovered, understood, and applied, is practical and productive. We are thankful for mathematicians and musicians and engineers.

Some invisible things are intelligible. Some invisible things are spiritual. Within God's creation are invisible powers and principalities, angels and demons, cherubim and seraphim, and Satan. There are times when the invisible, spiritual realm is manifest. It was revealed to Elijah and Elisha, Isaiah and Ezekiel, and Paul and John. But normally this realm is veiled.

Veiled, but present and real and contested, which is why Paul exhorts us: "be strong in the Lord and in the strength of his might. Put

---

10 Composed by Maltbie D. Babcock (1901).

on the whole armour of God, that you may be able to stand against the schemes of the devil" (Eph 6:10-11). We can stand because we are strong in Christ.

Standing is the posture of prayer in Scripture. In prayer we are strengthened to stand, which is why Paul calls on us to stay alert and persevere in prayer: "praying at all times in the Spirit" (Eph 6:18). In prayer, we draw near the throne of grace. We stand in prayer because we recognize that we are in God's presence. In the light of his presence and grace, we recognize the armour he has given us. In the light of his presence and grace, we see our invisible enemies and stand in the strength of his might, the might of the One who made all things, visible and invisible. They are no threat to him. He made them. We do not need to be afraid, for he has redeemed us. He stands with us and he is for us:

> If God is for us, who can be against us? ... No, in all these things we are more than conquerors through him who loved us. For I am sure that neither death nor life, nor angels nor rulers, nor things present nor things to come, nor powers, nor height nor depth, nor anything else in all creation, will be able to separate us from the love of God in Christ Jesus our Lord." (Rom 8:31, 37-39)

2
We Believe in God the Son

We believe in one Lord, Jesus Christ, the only-begotten Son of God, eternally begotten from the Father, Light from Light, true God from true God, begotten not made, the same being with the Father, through whom all things were made.

One Lord
When we confess that Jesus is Lord, we are confessing his divinity, his redemption, and his sovereignty.

First, when we confess that Jesus is Lord, we confess his divinity. The God of Abraham, Isaac, and Jacob revealed himself to Moses as "Yahweh" – "I Am Who I Am" (Ex 3:14). When the New Testament writers quote the Old Testament, they usually quote the Greek translation of the Scriptures, where the divine name "Yahweh" is translated as *Kurios* (Lord). Thus, in our English translations of the Hebrew Scriptures, "Yahweh" is translated as "Lord" (in small caps, indicating the divine name).

We hear the divine name in Israel's confession: "Hear, O Israel: The Lord our God, the Lord is one" (Deut 6:4). In Isaiah 45, Yahweh testifies, "I am the LORD, there is no other" (vv.5, 6, 18). He, and he alone creates and rules all things (vv.7, 8, 14, 18) and he alone saves (vv.15-17, 21-22). And he declares, "to me every knee shall bow, every tongue shall swear allegiance" (v.23).

Deuteronomy 6 and Isaiah 45 declare that the LORD and the LORD alone is God: Creator, Ruler, and Saviour. The Apostle Paul cites and applies both these passages to Jesus. He applies Deuteronomy 6 to Jesus in 1 Corinthians 8:6: "for us there is one God, the Father, from whom are all things and for whom we exist, and one Lord, Jesus Christ, through whom are all things and through whom we exist." And he applies Isaiah 45 to Jesus in Philippians 2:10-11: "at the name of Jesus every knee should bow, in heaven and on earth and under the earth, and every tongue confess that Jesus Christ is Lord, to the glory of God the Father." When we confess that Jesus is Lord, we confess his divinity. He is Yahweh. He is God.

Second, when we confess that Jesus is Lord, we confess his redemption. He has purchased us for himself: "You are not your own, for you were bought with a price" (1 Cor 6:19-20). The price was his life, which he gave as a ransom for sinners. When we confess that Jesus is Lord, we confess that we belong to him, because he has ransomed us. The LORD is our LORD and we are his. "Therefore," Paul exhorts, "glorify God in your body" (1 Cor 6:20), because "the body is not meant for sexual immorality, but for the Lord" (1 Cor 6:14).

Third, when we confess that Jesus is Lord, we confess his sovereignty. The Roman Caesars gave themselves the title "Lord." *Kurios* was stamped on Roman coins and inscribed on monuments throughout the empire. The early Christians declared, "Jesus is Lord." He is King of kings and Lord of lords. Many have claimed to be lord throughout history. But Caesars, Kaisers, and Czars are not lord. We believe in one Lord, Jesus Christ. He alone is the "ruler of the kings of the earth" (Rev 1:5) and he is seated "at the right hand of the Majesty on high" (Heb 1:3), "far above all rule and authority and power and dominion, and above every name that is named, not only in this age but also in the one to come" (Eph 1:21). To him be glory forever! Amen.

Jesus

We confess in the Nicene Creed that "we believe in one Lord, Jesus Christ." The one Lord is named, "Jesus." The angel Gabriel announced to the virgin Mary, "And behold, you will conceive in your womb and bear a son, and you shall call his name Jesus" (Luke 1:31). Jesus in Greek is the same name as Joshua in Hebrew, which means "Yahweh saves." The meaning of his name is brought out in the angel's command to Joseph, "Joseph, son of David, do not fear to take Mary as your wife, for that which is conceived in her is from the Holy Spirit. She will bear a son, and you shall call his name Jesus, for he will save his people from their sins" (Matt 1:21-22).

God created human beings, male and female, in his image and likeness to rule and serve in his creation as kings and priests (Gen 1:26-28; 2:15; Ps 8). The first man and woman, Adam and Eve, listened to the deceiving counsel of the serpent and disobeyed God's command not to eat from the tree of the knowledge of good and evil. In Adam, humanity fell.

David speaks for every man and woman when he confesses,

> "I was brought forth in iniquity,
>   and in sin did my mother conceive me" (Ps 51:5)

and again,

> "God looks down from heaven
>   on the children of man
> to see if there are any who understand,
>   who seek after God.
> They have all fallen away;
>   together they have become corrupt;
> there is none who does good,
>   not even one" (Ps 53:2-3).

Every man and woman is born corrupted in sin and under God's just condemnation: "for all have sinned and fall short of the glory of God and the wages of sin is death" (Rom 3:23; 6:23). The sinful corruption of men and women is manifest in our idolatry, which leads to all manner of sinful attitudes and actions, which transgress God's commandments (Ps 115:1-8; Rom 1:18-32). We are sinners, corrupted by sin and condemned for our transgressions. We need salvation.

We believe in one Lord, Jesus Christ. He is named Jesus because he saves his people from their sins. He and he alone is the Saviour, as the Apostle Peter proclaimed, "and there is salvation in no one else, for there is no other name under heaven given among men by which we must be saved" (Acts 4:12). There is salvation in no one or nothing else, no political party, no economic theory, no social policy, no educational curriculum, and no religious movement.

The only name under heaven by which sinners may be saved is Jesus. He alone is Saviour and by faith in him alone are sinners saved.

Christ

The word "Christ" means "anointed." In Hebrew, "Christ" or "anointed one" is "Messiah." Consider what Luke the Evangelist reports in Luke 4:16-21:

> And he came to Nazareth, where he had been brought up. And as was his custom, he went to the synagogue on the Sabbath day, and he stood up to read. And the scroll of the prophet Isaiah was given to him. He unrolled the scroll and found the place where it was written,
>
> > "The Spirit of the Lord is upon me,
> >   because he has anointed me
> >   to proclaim good news to the poor.
> > He has sent me to proclaim liberty to the captives
> >   and recovering of sight to the blind,
> >   to set at liberty those who are oppressed,
> > to proclaim the year of the Lord's favour."

And he rolled up the scroll and gave it back to the attendant and sat down. And the eyes of all in the synagogue were fixed on him. And he began to say to them, "Today this Scripture has been fulfilled in your hearing."

Jesus is the Christ, promised by the prophet and anointed by the Spirit.

The confession that Jesus is the Christ was at the heart of the apostles' preaching: "And every day, in the temple and from house to house, they did not cease teaching and preaching Jesus as the Christ" (Acts 5:42). While there is much to say about the significance of this title, I find the summary statement in the Heidelberg Catechism helpful. While we think of anointing primarily with reference to kings, the catechism reminds us that prophets and priests were also anointed.

> Question 31: Why is He called "Christ," that is, "Anointed?"
>
> Answer: Because he has been ordained by God the Father and has been anointed with the Holy Spirit to be our chief prophet and teacher who fully reveals to us the secret counsel and will of God concerning our deliverance; our only high priest who has delivered us by the one sacrifice of his body, and who continually pleads our cause with the Father; and our eternal king who governs us by his Word and Spirit, and who guards us and keeps us in the freedom he has won for us.[1]

We read in Acts that followers of Jesus were called Christians. The catechism asks a follow up question:

> Question 32: But why are you called a Christian?
> Answer: Because by faith I am a member of Christ,

---

1 *The Heidelberg Catechism*, 21.

and so I share in his anointing. I am anointed to confess his name, to present myself to him a living sacrifice of thanks, to strive with a good conscience against sin and the devil in this life, and afterward to reign with Christ over all creation, for all eternity.[2]

Jesus is the Christ, the Messiah. The Spirit joins believers to Christ, so we are in Christ and, therefore, Christians.

The Only-Begotten Son of God, Eternally Begotten from the Father
The ancient world, like many cultures today, was polytheistic. To pagan ears, there was nothing too surprising in the Christian confession that Jesus was divine. So were men like Julius Caesar and Augustus. The Nicene Creed articulates our faith in the divinity of Christ in a way that distinguishes his divinity from polytheistic notions of divinity and in a way that distils biblical language concerning God. After we confess that "we believe in one Lord, Jesus Christ" there is a string of phrases intended to articulate the full divinity of the Son of God and his unique relationship to God the Father: "the only-begotten Son of God, eternally begotten from the Father, Light from Light, true God from true God, begotten, not made, the same being with the Father."

The Son is begotten, he is only-begotten, and he is eternally begotten. "Begotten" is an old word, rarely used in day-to-day conversation. It refers to the generation of life from a father. You are begotten from your father. Thus, in the King James Version of Adam's genealogy, the words "begat" and "begotten" are repeated. Adam begat Seth; Seth was begotten from Adam. Seth's life is from his father Adam.

God's Word testifies that the Son is begotten from the Father (John 1:14, 18; Heb 1:5). God the Father is unbegotten. God the Son is begotten from the Father. This means the life of the Son is from the Father. This is what Jesus himself declares in John 5:26: "For as the

---

[2] *The Heidelberg Catechism*, 21.

Father has life in himself, so he has granted the Son also to have life in himself."

The Nicene Creed adds two qualifiers: the Son is the only-begotten and he is eternally begotten.[3] First, he is the only-begotten Son of God (John 1:14, 18). God the Father does not have two sons (the Spirit is not begotten) or three sons or a million sons. He has one Son, the Only-Begotten. In Christ, we are adopted as sons. We have received the Spirit of adoption. We are co-heirs with Christ. His Father is our Father. But Christ alone is the only-begotten Son from the Father.

Second, the Son is eternally begotten from the Father. The word "begotten" implies a beginning, a coming into existence. Seth did not exist before he was begotten from Adam. This is not the case with God the Son. He was eternally begotten. He has his life from the Father, but he is without beginning or end. The Father has always been the Father and the Son has always been the Son. In the early fourth century, the Arians used to sing about the Son, "There was a time when he was not." They sang lies. The Son is eternally begotten.

The Son is the only-begotten Son of God, eternally begotten from the Father. He has his life from the Father. His life is eternal and the Father sent him to give us this eternal life:

> Truly, truly, I say to you, whoever hears my word and believes him who sent me has eternal life. He does not come into judgment, but has passed from death to life. Truly, truly, I say to you, an hour is coming, and is now here, when the dead will hear the voice of the Son of God, and those who hear will live. For as the Father has life in himself, so he has granted the Son also to have life in himself. (John 5:24-26)

Light from Light, True God from True God

We confess that the only- and eternally-begotten Son is "Light from

---

3 "Eternally" translates a phrase in Greek which is literally translated "before all ages."

Light." This phrase affirms the unique transcendence of the Son. The Apostle John writes that at the heart of the Gospel message is the declaration that "God is light, and in him there is no darkness at all" (1 John 1:5). The Apostle Paul writes that our Lord Jesus Christ "dwells in unapproachable light, whom no one has ever seen or can see" (1 Tim 6:16). John and Paul are referring to the uncreated Light of God. In his divine being, God is unapproachable and incomprehensible. He is holy. This does not mean we cannot know him and have communion with him, but we will never fully know him, as he fully knows us.

We confess that the Son is "Light from Light," which means he shares in the transcendence and holiness of God the Father. He dwells in unapproachable light and he is Light from Light. Just as light is visible, perceived, and received because of its radiance, so the Son is "the radiance of the glory of God" (Heb 1:3). By the light of the sun, we see the sun; by the light of the Son, we see God. As Jesus said to Philip, "whoever has seen me, has seen the Father" (John 14:9).

Thus, David praises Jesus when he sings, "in your light do we see light" (Ps 36:9). He is Light from Light. In our church, we bless one another every Sunday with these words, "the LORD bless you and keep you; the LORD make his face to shine upon you and be gracious to you" (Numbers 6:24-25). This blessing is fulfilled and received in Jesus. Our Lord Jesus Christ is the radiance of the glory of God, who "has shone in our hearts to give us the light of the knowledge of the glory of God in the face of Jesus Christ" (2 Cor 4:6). Jesus is God's face shining upon us.

The Son is "Light from Light, true God from true God." Again, remember what Jesus said to Philip at the last supper. Philip said to him, "Lord, show us the Father, and it is enough for us." Jesus said to him, "Have I been with you so long, and you still do not know me, Philip? Whoever has seen me has seen the Father" (John 14:8-9). Whoever has seen Jesus has seen the Father. Whoever knows the Son knows the Father. Whoever truly knows Jesus truly knows God. Whoever does not know Jesus does not know God.

Consider three implications of our confession that the Son is "true

God from true God." First, God is known in Christ and in Christ alone. Hence, the exclusive claims of Christ and the Gospel. He is the Way.

Second, theology is centred on Christ. As we come to know him, we come to know God. He is the Truth.

Third, knowing him is not learning about him, the acquisition of the right concepts and terminology. Knowing him is knowing God and knowing God is eternal life. As Jesus prayed at that last supper, "And this is eternal life, that they know you the only true God, and Jesus Christ whom you have sent" (John 17:3). And as John writes in his first letter, "And we know that the Son of God has come and has given us understanding, so that we may know him who is true; and we are in him who is true, in his Son Jesus Christ. He is the true God and eternal life" (1 John 5:20). Knowing the Son is eternal life. Because he is true God from true God, he is the Life.

The Son is true God from true God. He is the Way, the Truth, and the Life (John 14:6).

Begotten, Not Made

I have already considered the term "begotten." The phrase "begotten, not made" provides a clarification: when we say that the Son is begotten, we in no way imply that he is made. Seth was begotten from Adam, but he was also made. The Son of God is eternally begotten from the Father, but he is not made. The Son is not a creature; he is Creator. He is not made; he is Maker.

Many people in the ancient Mediterranean world held a platonic worldview, which divided the world into an intelligible realm and a sensible realm. They viewed the intelligible realm as eternal and uncreated and the sensible realm as temporal and created. For Plato, there is a great dividing line between the sensible and intelligible realm which must be traversed. Knowledge of the true, the good, and the beautiful requires access to the intelligible realm, which is restricted by our experience of the sensible realm. For Plato, salvation means transcending the sensible realm through enlightenment and knowledge of the intelligible realm.

But we confess that God the Father is the "Maker of heaven and earth, of all things visible and invisible." In other words, he is the Maker of both the intelligible realm and sensible realm. When we confess that the Son is "begotten, not made" we are confessing that with the Father, he is the Maker of heaven and earth, of all things visible and invisible. Contrary to Plato, salvation does not require enlightenment but redemption and reconciliation with God through forgiveness and cleansing of sin. We cannot reconcile or redeem ourselves. But there is good news. Jump ahead in the Nicene Creed: the eternal Son, who is begotten, not made, "for us men and for our salvation . . . became man." As the Apostle Paul testifies, "when the fullness of time had come, God sent forth his Son, born of woman" (Gal 4:4). And again, "for there is one God, and there is one mediator between God and men, the man Christ Jesus, who gave himself as a ransom for all" (1 Tim 2:5-6).

The Same Being with the Father

The Son is "the same being with the Father." The Greek word translated "same being" is *homoousios*, which is a compound word: *homo* "same" and *ousia* "substance, essence, or being." Some English translations render the word "same substance" or "same essence" or "constubstantial."

The word *homoousios* is not found in Scripture. Thus far the Creed has used biblical language to confess the full divinity of the Son, but with this phrase, a non-biblical word is used. As we saw in the introduction, the use of this word *homoousios* was the source of much controversy in the fourth century; however, when the Creed was revised at the Council of Constantinople in 381, the word remained. The Son is "the same being with the Father."

The word *homoousios* expresses the essential unity of the Father and the Son and the Spirit. God's attributes are essential. For example, God does not have or acquire righteousness. He is righteous in his very being. He *is* righteousness. The Son and the Spirit are of the same being as the Father, which means the Son and the Spirit share one and the same holiness, life, knowledge, wisdom, will, power, authority, and glory with the Father.

This is why the Creed goes on to confess that the Holy Spirit is worshipped and glorified with the Father. The term *homoousios* guards the integrity of our worship. We confess that the Son is "the same being with the Father" because all creation sings: "To him who sits on the throne and to the Lamb be blessing and honour and glory and might for ever and ever!" (Rev 5:13)

Through Whom All Things Were Made
Following a series of phrases that articulate the full divinity of the Son, the Creed turns our attention from the Son's relationship with the Father to the Son's relationship to creation and to us. Quoting John 1:3, we confess, "through him all things were made" or "through him all things came to be." Our confession here elaborates what we have already confessed concerning God the Father, who is the "Maker of heaven and earth, of all things visible and invisible." The Father is Creator and the Son is Creator. (The Spirit's identity as Creator is later acknowledged when we confess that he is "the Lord and giver of life.")

The opening verses of John's Gospel echo the opening words of Genesis. The declaration that "through him all things came to be" in John 1:3 corresponds with Genesis 1:3: "And God said, 'Let there be light,' and there was light." The Son of God is the Word of God. Through him, all things came to be. We need to account for the reference to "all things." All things means all things, such as a beehive, a bird's nest, a child's sandcastle, and Beethoven's 7th Symphony. All things – sandcastles and symphonies – came to be through him.

This confession implies a Christ-centered view of the cosmos and a Christ-oriented teleology, which the Apostle Paul captures in his hymn, "For by him all things were created, in heaven and on earth, visible and invisible, whether thrones or dominions or rulers or authorities—all things were created through him and for him. And he is before all things, and in him all things hold together" (Col 1:16-17).

Think for moment about the staggering implications of these two verses for how you view the world and your day-to-day life in it.

On a personal level, the "all things" of John 1:3 and Colossians 1:16 includes you and me. You came to be through him and you are for him, which is why Augustine confesses to God, "you have made us for yourself and our hearts are restless, until they find their rest in you" (*Confessions* I.1.1).[4] And the same Word, through whom and for whom are all things, summons, "Come to me, all you who labour and are heavy laden, and I will give you rest" (Matt 11:28).

---

4   *Saint Augustine: Confessions*, trans. Henry Chadwick, Oxford World's Classics (Oxford: Oxford University Press, 1992), 3.

3
For Us Men and for Our Salvation

For us men and for our salvation he came down from heaven; he was incarnate by the Holy Spirit and the Virgin Mary, and became man. He was crucified for us under Pontius Pilate; he suffered, died, and was buried. On the third day he rose again according to the Scriptures; he ascended into heaven and is seated at the right hand of the Father. He will come again in glory to judge the living and the dead, and his kingdom will have no end.

For Us Men and for Our Salvation
There are three articles in the Nicene Creed: on the Father, the Son, and the Holy Spirit. The second article on the Son is the longest. The first part of the second article articulates the identity of the Son and his relationship to the Father; however, the last phrase of that first part turns our attention to the Son's relationship to creation. The second part of the second article addresses his relationship to us and our salvation.

The Nicene Creed is a theological confession. It is about God. It is also a soteriological confession: we confess what the "One Lord, Jesus

Christ, the only-begotten Son of God" has done "for us men and for our salvation." The Creed is a summary of what the Apostle Paul calls "the doctrine of God our Saviour" (Titus 2:10). God our Saviour is the God who "for us men and for our salvation, came down from heaven."

"For us." This short prepositional phrase reorients our whole theological outlook. God is for us. We know God is for us because the Son of God came down from heaven, was incarnate and became man, was crucified, suffered, and was buried, and on the third day rose again according to the Scriptures.

He is for us because he loves us. Again, the Apostle Paul declares in Titus 3:4 that the appearance of the Son of God in the flesh was the appearance of the "lovingkindness of God." Lovingkindness translates the Greek word *philanthrōpia*. Jesus is the manifestation of God's love for humanity. God so loved the world he sent his only Son.

Paul contemplates the implications of such divine *philanthrōpia*: "I consider that the sufferings of this present time are not worth comparing with the glory that is to be revealed to us" and "that for those who love God all things work for good," because "if God is for us, who can be against us? He who did not spare his own Son but gave him up for us all, how will he not also with him graciously give us all things?" (Rom 8:18, 28, 31-32).

Finally, remember that "us" includes you. If God is for us, then he is for me. I pray that you can testify with the Apostle Paul, "the life I now live in the flesh I live by faith in the Son of God, who loved me and gave himself for me" (Gal 2:20b).

Came Down from Heaven

God our Saviour is the God who "for us men and for our salvation, came down from heaven." How do we know that God is for us? He came down from heaven. God is a God who condescends for sinners. He came down to find Adam and Eve when they sinned in the garden (Gen 3:8). He came down to make a covenant with Abraham (Gen 15). He came down to deliver Israel from slavery in Egypt (Ex 3). He came down to deliver us from our bondage to sin and Satan (Heb 2).

For us men and for our salvation he came down from heaven.

When the Son of God came down, he did not simply come down from heaven to earth. He came down from heaven to us, miserable sinners, children of wrath, exiled and alienated from God, at enmity with God, dead in our trespasses and sins, subject to sin, death, and Satan (Eph 2:1-3). He came down from heaven to the depths of our sin and darkness. He found us there. He bore our sin and our shame and our condemnation. He called us by name, he took us to himself, and he is bringing us as sons to glory (Heb 2:10).

Finally, as the writer of Hebrews reminds us, by coming down from heaven, the Son of God became our high priest: "Therefore he had to be made like his brothers in every respect, so that he might become a merciful and faithful high priest in the service of God, to make propitiation for the sins of the people" (Heb 2:17). Our high priest, who came down from heaven, is now seated at the right hand of the Majesty on high:

> Since then we have a great high priest who has passed through the heavens, Jesus, the Son of God, let us hold fast our confession. For we do not have a high priest who is unable to sympathize with our weaknesses, but one who in every respect has been tempted as we are, yet without sin. Let us then with confidence draw near to the throne of grace, that we may receive mercy and find grace to help in time of need. (Heb 4:14-16)

He Was Incarnate

How do we know that God is for us? God our Saviour came down from heaven and "was incarnate." The word "incarnate" means to be "enfleshed." It refers to our material substance. Squeeze your forearm. You are squeezing flesh. As you know, flesh gets bruised, tired, strained, and weak. One day you will die and your flesh will decay and return to dust. The word "flesh" in Scripture points beyond our physical flesh. It refers more broadly to our weakness, our need, our mortality, our corruptibility.

The Son of God did not simply come down to us. He was incarnate. Enfleshed. As the Apostle John declares in John 1:14: "The Word became flesh and dwelt among us." He did not sin, but he took on the weakness and vulnerability and mortality of our flesh. As the Apostle Paul writes, he "made himself nothing, taking the form of a servant, being born in the likeness of men. And being found in human form, he humbled himself by becoming obedient to the point of death, even death on a cross" (Phil 2:7-8).

John not only says that "the Word became flesh and dwelt among us," he adds, "and we have seen his glory, glory as of the only Son from the Father." Flesh is not associated with glory. In fact, in the ancient world it was associated with dishonour and shame. But we see the glory of the eternal Son in the flesh of the Son. And in his glory, we see the hope of glory. Paul, in the same letter to the Philippians, goes on to write, "But our citizenship is in heaven, and from it we await a Saviour, the Lord Jesus Christ, who will transform our lowly body to be like his glorious body, by the power that enables him even to subject all things to himself" (Phil 3:20-21).

The Son of God was incarnate. He suffered in the flesh and was raised in glory in the flesh. So, yes, when you squeeze your forearm, you are squeezing flesh that will one day decay and return dust. But you are also squeezing flesh that will one day be raised and transformed in resurrection glory: "It is sown in dishonour; it is raised in glory" (1 Cor 15:43).

He Was Incarnate by the Holy Spirit

He came down from heaven and he was incarnate "by the Holy Spirit and the Virgin Mary." The Son of God was incarnate by the Holy Spirit. When the angel Gabriel announced to Mary that she would conceive and bear a son, she asked him, "How will this be, since I am a virgin?" And the angel replied, "The Holy Spirit will come upon you, and the power of the Most High will overshadow you" (Luke 1:35). The Son of God became flesh in the womb of Mary by the Holy Spirit.

The angel's answer to Mary reminds us of Genesis 1:2: "The earth was without form and void, and darkness was over the face of the deep. And the Spirit of God was hovering over the face of the waters." The state of the earth in Genesis 1 reflects the state of Mary's womb in Luke 1: empty, dark, nothing formed. Just as the Spirit of God hovered over the face of the deep, so he overshadowed Mary.

As it was in the beginning, so it is again in the womb of Mary. Just as the Spirit forms life out of the empty darkness of the virgin earth, so he forms life out of the empty darkness of the virgin womb. The Word who was with God in the beginning, when the Spirit hovered over the face of the deep, became flesh and tabernacled among us, when the Spirit of God overshadowed Mary. A new beginning.

This new beginning promises us a new beginning. He became flesh by the Holy Spirit so that we, who are conceived in sin, may be born again by the same Spirit (John 3:6-7).

This new beginning also orients us to a new end. The same Lord Jesus Christ, the only-begotten Son of God, who was incarnate by the Holy Spirit and who suffered and died for sin, was raised by the Spirit on the third day. The same Spirit who raised Jesus from the dead will give life to our mortal bodies (Rom 8:11; 1 Pet 3:18). Thus, we can sing:

> Holy Spirit, living breath of God
> Breathe new life into my willing soul
> Bring the presence of the risen Lord
> To renew my heart and make me whole
> Cause Your Word to come alive in me
> Give me faith for what I cannot see
> Give me passion for Your purity
> Holy Spirit, breathe new life in me.[1]

---

1 Keith Getty and Stuart Townend, "Holy Spirit, Living Breath of God" (2005).

He Was Incarnate by the Virgin Mary

There is not only a resonance between Genesis 1 and Luke 1, between the Spirit's presence and work in creation and the Spirit's presence and work in the incarnation, there is also a resonance between Genesis 2 and Luke 1. In the beginning, when no seed had yet been planted in the earth, God formed Adam of dust from the virgin ground (Genesis 2:5-7). In the fullness of time, the Son of God, the Last Adam, was incarnate by the virgin Mary.

There is a further resonance (or, better, a dissonance) between Genesis 3 and Luke 1. Whereas Eve was deceived and disobeyed God, Mary believed and obeyed God: "Behold, I am the servant of the Lord; let it be to me according to your word" (Luke 1:38). In Genesis 3, there is the fall of humanity and the curse. In Luke 1, the Son of God comes down and there is blessing: "And Elizabeth was filled with the Holy Spirit, and she exclaimed with a loud cry, 'Blessed are you among women, and blessed is the fruit of your womb! And why is this granted to me that the mother of my Lord should come to me?'" (Luke 1:41-44).

Elizabeth, filled with the Spirit, calls Mary blessed. We should call her blessed: "for behold, from now on all generations shall call me blessed" (Luke 1:48). Elizabeth, filled with the Holy Spirit, testifies that Mary is the mother of the Lord. The Son of God, eternally begotten from the Father, Light from Light, true God from true God, of the same being as the Father, was incarnate from the virgin Mary. In 451, the Council of Chalcedon elaborated this point in the Nicene Creed, confessing that one and the same Son of God, our Lord Jesus Christ is "begotten before all ages from God the Father as regards his divinity, and in the last days the same for us and for our salvation from Mary the virgin God-bearer (*Theotokos*) as regards his humanity." He is "perfect in divinity and perfect in humanity" and he is "truly God and truly man."[2]

To say that Mary is the Mother of God or the God-bearer is to

---

2   *Creeds & Confessions of Faith in the Christian Tradition*, 180, 181.

confess that her son Jesus is the Son of God. She is the mother of the Lord. To call her the Mother of God does not magnify her, it magnifies the Lord. And with her, we sing:

> My soul magnifies the Lord,
>   and my spirit rejoices in God my Saviour,
>   for he has looked on the humble estate of his servant.
> For behold, from now on all generations will call me blessed;
>   for he who is mighty has done great things for me,
>   and holy is his name. (Luke 1:46-49)

And Became Man
The Son of God became man. In the words of the Definition of Chalcedon (AD 451), he is "perfect in divinity and perfect in humanity, the same truly God and truly man." We carry the corruption of sin. We are not perfect in humanity. He is perfect in humanity and truly man. In Jesus we see humanity "holy, innocent, unstained" (Heb 7:26). When we think about the humanity of the Son of God, we need to avoid two errors: (1) we cannot think or suggest that the Son is not perfect in humanity and truly man and (2) we cannot think or suggest that in Christ, there are two persons or two sons, one human and one divine.

First, we cannot think or suggest that the Son is not perfect in humanity and truly man. In the 4th century, Apollinarius of Laodicea taught that in the incarnation, the Son of God occupied the rational soul or mind of Jesus of Nazareth. The Word assumed human flesh, but not a human mind. Gregory of Nazianzus, helps us to see the error in Apollinarius's thinking:

> What He has not assumed He has not healed; but that which is united to His Godhead is also saved. If only half an Adam had fallen then that which Christ assumes and heals might only be half as well; but if the whole of Adam's nature fell then it must be united to the whole nature of

the Begotten One, and so be saved as a whole. (*Letter* 101.5)[3]

Second, we cannot think or suggest that in the incarnation, there are two persons or sons, one human and one divine. Again, in the 4th century, Diodore of Tarsus taught that God the Son joined himself to Jesus of Nazareth, so that the incarnation is a union of two persons, the Son of God and the Son of Man. In the same letter I just quoted, Gregory helps us to see the error of Diodore's thinking: "Whoever imports two 'sons,' one from God the Father, a second from the mother, and not one and the same Son, loses the adoption promised to those who believe aright. Two natures there are, God and man, but not two 'sons'" (*Letter* 101.5).[4]

We need to avoid these two errors. The Council of Chalcedon articulates what we should affirm:

> One and the same Christ, Son, Lord, Only-begotten, acknowledged in two natures which undergo no confusion, no change, no division, no separation; at no point was the difference between the natures taken away though the union, but rather the property of both natures is preserved and comes together into a single person and single subsistent being; he is not parted or divided into two persons, but is one and the same only-begotten Son, God, Word, Lord Jesus Christ.[5]

The Son of God became man. He is perfect in humanity and truly man; he is perfect in divinity and truly God. There is only one "he," one person, a single subject, the Son of God. Leo the Great articulates this truth more poetically:

---

[3] Trans. John McGuckin, *Saint Cyril of Alexandria and the Christological Controversy* (Crestwood NY: SVS Press, 2004), 393.
[4] Trans. Wickham, *On God and Christ*, 157.
[5] *Creeds & Confessions of Faith in the Christian Tradition*, 181.

In this preservation, then, of the real quality of both natures [divine and human], both being united in one person, lowliness was taken on by majesty, weakness by strength, mortality by the immortal. And in order to pay the debt of our fallen state, inviolable nature was united to one capable of suffering so that (and this is the sort of reparation we needed) one and the same mediator between God and men, the man Jesus Christ, could die in the one nature and not die in the other. In the whole and perfect nature of the true man, then, the true God was born, complete in His own nature, complete in ours. (*Letter* 28.3)[6]

The Son of God became man for us men and for our salvation. He became man so that he could die.

He Was Crucified for Us under Pontius Pilate

After we confess his incarnation, that he came down from heaven and became man, the Creed leads us to the cross: "He was crucified for us under Pontius Pilate." In Genesis 3, after the Lord GOD curses the ground to bring thorns, he announces Adam's death: "to dust you will return." He clothes Adam and Eve. He declares, "Behold, the man" and then drives him out of the garden, to work the ground east of Eden (Gen 3:18-24). In the Gospel of John, Pontius Pilate presents Jesus, crowned with thorns and clothed in purple, and declares, "Behold, the man." But the chief priests and officers cry out, "Crucify him, crucify him!" and he is led out of the city to hang on a tree (John 19:5-6).

Jesus is the Last Adam, who "redeemed us from the curse of the law by becoming a curse for us—for it is written, 'Cursed is everyone who is hanged on a tree'" (Gal 3:13; Deut 21:22-23). When he was crucified

---

6 *St Leo the Great: Letters*, trans. Edmund Hunt, Fathers of the Church no.34 (New York: Catholic University of America Press, 1957), 95-96.

for us, he became a curse for us, "so that in Christ Jesus the blessing of Abraham might come to the Gentiles, so that we might receive the promised Spirit through faith" (Gal 3:14). From the accursed cross of Christ, the blessing of the Holy Spirit flows. Jesus himself promised this would happen:

> "If anyone thirsts, let him come to me and drink. Whoever believes in me, as the Scripture has said, 'Out of his heart will flow rivers of living water.'" Now this he said about the Spirit, whom those who believed in him were to receive, for as yet the Spirit had not been given, because Jesus was not yet glorified. (John 7:37-39)

As we read on in John's Gospel, we learn that Jesus is glorified on the cross, for he says at the beginning of passion week: "The hour has come for the Son of Man to be glorified. Truly, truly, I say to you, unless a grain of wheat falls into the earth and dies, it remains alone; but if it dies, it bears much fruit" (John 12:23-24).

He was crucified for us. He was cursed for us, hung on a tree for us, so that we may receive the blessing of the Holy Spirit. His death bears much fruit. His cross is a tree of life and he makes his blessings flow far as the curse is found.

Pontius Pilate, the first-century Roman governor of Judea, is named in the Nicene Creed. What's he doing there? His name reminds us that our faith is grounded in history. Our faith is not a philosophy or mythology. It's not an ethical system or a set of religious rituals and practices. No, we believe in one Lord Jesus Christ, the only-begotten Son of God, eternally begotten from the Father, Light from Light, true God from God, who for us men and for our salvation, came down from heaven, became man, and was crucified for us under Pontius Pilate. This happened, at a particular time and place, under the rule and decree of Pontius Pilate.

He Suffered

The Son of God suffered. We dare not let crucifixion become abstracted or reduced to a doctrinal concept or religious symbol. We cannot avoid the scandal and the suffering of the cross. Crucifixion was designed to inflict maximum suffering, both physical and psychological. It was designed to degrade and dehumanize. And it was not unique to the Romans but widely practiced in the ancient world among Persians, Indians, Assyrians, Scythians, Greeks, North Africans, Celts, Britons, and Germanic peoples. It was a universal expression of human depravity and barbarity.

The Son of God suffered crucifixion. He knew he would suffer and suffered willingly. Consider what we read in Hebrews 10:5-7 (citing Psalm 40:4-6):

> when Christ came into the world, he said,
> "Sacrifices and offerings you have not desired,
> but a body have you prepared for me;
> in burnt offerings and sin offerings
> you have taken no pleasure.
> Then I said, 'Behold, I have come to do your will, O God,
> as it is written of me in the scroll of the book.'"

The Son of God says, "A body have you prepared for me." He was incarnate. He became man. And he says, "I have come to do your will, O God, as it is written of me in the scroll of the book."

There are many passages in the Hebrew Scriptures that announce the will of God for the Messiah, including suffering in his body. For example, the Messiah hears and accepts his call to suffer in Isaiah 50:5-6:

> The Lord GOD has opened my ear,
> and I was not rebellious;
> I turned not backwards.
> I gave my back to those who strike,

> and my cheeks to those who pull out the beard;
> I hid not my face
> > from disgrace and spitting.

When Peter declares, "You are the Christ!" Jesus "began to teach them that the Son of Man must suffer many things" (Mark 8:30-31). He heard and obeyed the call to suffer. He was not rebellious. He did not turn back and he did not hide his face. He was obedient to the point of death, even death on a cross (Phil 2:8).

He suffered for us and for our sins: "For Christ also suffered once for sins, the righteous for the unrighteous, that he might bring us to God" (1 Pet 3:18). The severity of his suffering reveals the severity of our sins. His suffering was ugly, vile, and abhorrent because our sin is abhorrent, vile, and ugly.

> Bearing shame and scoffing rude,
> in my place condemned he stood,
> sealed my pardon with his blood:
> Hallelujah, what a Savior![7]

And Was Buried

The crucified and dead body of the Son of God was buried. The words God spoke to the first Adam are now directed to him: "By the sweat of your face you shall eat bread, till you return to the ground, for out of it you were taken; for you are dust, and to dust you shall return" (Genesis 3:19). As the author of Hebrews puts it, "by the grace of God he tasted death for everyone" (Heb 2:9). His burial confirms his vicarious death for sinners. The wages of sin is death. Having borne our sin, he suffered our death (Rom 6:23). His burial confirms that God has set aside the record of debt that stood against us with its legal demands (death), nailing it to the cross (Col 2:13-14).

---

[7] Philip P. Bliss, "Man of Sorrows, What a Name" (1875).

His burial is also a great comfort to us in our death. Our Lord tasted death. He is our pioneer, who has gone ahead of us into death, and through death, he is bringing many sons to glory (Heb 2:10). This is why David could pray in Psalm 23:4: "Even though I walk through the valley of the shadow of death, I will fear no evil; for you are with me." He is with us when we die and he brings us to himself in death. And so, we can say with Paul that death cannot separate us from the love of God in Jesus Christ (Rom 8:38-39).

And when you die, he lays his right hand on you and says, "Fear not, I am the first and the last, and the living one. I died, and behold I am alive for evermore, and I have the keys of Death and Hades" (Rev 1:17-18). He was buried, but death could not hold him, he loosed the pangs of death (Acts 2:24). God raised him from the dead on the third day. Because the grave could not hold him, the grave cannot hold us. Just as he was raised on the third day, so we will be raised on the last day.

On the Third Day He Rose Again

The burial of the crucified Son of God marks the low point in the Creed's dramatic plotline. From here we ascend: "On the third day he rose again according to the Scriptures." On the third day, he rose again. He was not resuscitated from the dead, like Lazarus. He was resurrected from the dead. Lazarus was raised and died again. He still awaits his resurrection. Jesus was resurrected on the third day.

Resurrection is not simply resuscitation or being restored to life. The Apostle Paul makes it clear in 1 Corinthians 15 that resurrection is transformation and glorification.

First, resurrection is transformation:

> Behold! I tell you a mystery. We shall not all sleep, but we shall all be changed, in a moment, in the twinkling of an eye, at the last trumpet. For the trumpet will sound, and the dead will be raised imperishable, and we shall be changed. For this perishable body must put on the

imperishable, and this mortal body must put on immortality. (1 Cor 15:51-53)

Second, resurrection is glorification:

> There are heavenly bodies and earthly bodies, but the glory of the heavenly is of one kind, and the glory of the earthly is of another. There is one glory of the sun, and another glory of the moon, and another glory of the stars; for star differs from star in glory. So is it with the resurrection of the dead. What is sown is perishable; what is raised is imperishable. It is sown in dishonour; it is raised in glory. It is sown in weakness; it is raised in power. It is sown a natural body; it is raised a spiritual body. (1 Cor 15:40-44)

Our Lord was raised in power and glory. And his resurrection on the third day is the firstfruits of our resurrection:

> In fact Christ has been raised from the dead, the firstfruits of those who have fallen asleep ... But each in his own order: Christ the firstfruits, then at his coming those who belong to Christ. (1 Cor 15:20, 23)

Because Christ was raised on the third day, we have the hope of resurrection on the last day, when he comes. He is the Resurrection and the Life. Because we belong to him, we can say with the apostles and prophets: "Death is swallowed up in victory. O death, where is your victory? O death, where is your sting?" (1 Cor 15:53-54; Is 25:8; Hos 13:14).

He Rose Again According to the Scriptures

In the Gospel of John, we read that the Peter and John, even when they saw the empty tomb, "did not understand the Scripture, that he must rise from the dead" (John 20:9). The resurrection of the Son of God on the third day must be understood according to the Scriptures, that is, according to the witness of the prophets and the apostles (Acts 10:39-43). In the closing verses of Luke's Gospel, the risen Lord Jesus says to his disciples:

> "These are my words that I spoke to you while I was still with you, that everything written about me in the Law of Moses and the Prophets and the Psalms must be fulfilled." Then he opened their minds to understand the Scriptures, and said to them, "Thus it is written, that the Christ should suffer and on the third day rise from the dead, and that repentance and forgiveness of sins should be proclaimed in his name to all nations, beginning from Jerusalem. You are witnesses of these things." (Luke 24:44-48)

As we read on in the Acts of the Apostles, the apostles will cite Scriptures from the Old Testament that prophesy Jesus's resurrection. For example, both Peter and Paul quote Psalm 16:10 in their Gospel preaching (Acts 2:27; 13:35): "for you will not abandon my soul to Hades, nor let your Holy One see corruption."

But when we confess that the Son of God "was raised on the third day according to the Scriptures" there is more in view than the fulfillment of specific prophesies. We are confessing that whole narrative of Scripture points to and is fulfilled in Jesus's resurrection. And we are confessing that we can only understand the resurrection of Jesus within the narrative of Scripture. Peter and John witnessed the empty tomb and met the risen Lord Jesus Christ on the third day, but they did not yet understand the Scripture. The risen Lord Jesus appointed the apostles as witnesses of the resurrection (Luke 24:45), but only after he opened the Scriptures and opened their minds to understand the Scriptures (Luke 24:48).

The apostles proclaimed the Gospel of Jesus's death and resurrection according to the Scriptures (1 Cor 15:3-4). We can only know the meaning of Jesus's death and resurrection if we understand the Scriptures. To help us see that the whole narrative of Scripture points to Jesus's death and resurrection, I want to highlight some of the death and resurrection plot points in the biblical story of redemption.

First, we can see the theme of life out of death in Genesis and Exodus. "There was evening and there was morning" (Gen 1). The day begins with darkness and ends with light. The passage of time moves from sleeping to waking, a daily death and resurrection. In the garden of Eden, Adam falls into a deep sleep. It's almost as if he dies, and from his side, Eve, the mother of the living, is made (Gen 2). He awakes from his deep sleep to meet her.

While Eve is the mother of the living, the wives of the Patriarchs have barren wombs. And, yet, from the dead womb of Sarah, Isaac is born, and from the dead womb of Rebekah, Jacob is born, and from the dead womb of Rachel, Joseph is born (Gen 11:30; 25:21; 29:31).

When God tested Abraham by asking him to sacrifice his only son Isaac, Abraham believed that God, who had already brought Isaac's life out of death, would raise him from the dead (Gen 22:5; Heb 11:19).

When God reveals himself to Moses in the burning bush, he gives him three signs to verify his divine presence and commissioning (Ex 4). All three signs signify life from death: his wooden staff become a live snake, his hand is turned leprous and dead and then made clean and alive, and water from Nile is turned into blood, which is life.

Second, we see the theme of life out of death in the biblical history of redemption. Because of Adam's trespass, there is death, enmity with the serpent, and the ground is cursed. Who will atone for sin, conquer death, crush the serpent, and reverse the curse? As you read through Genesis, there are moments when you think it may be Enoch or Noah or Abraham or Joseph; however, as we read in Hebrews 11:13: "these all died."

But there is a promise of one who will suffer and die, make atonement for sin, defeat death, crush the serpent, and make his blessings flow far as the curse is found. His death and resurrection is announced in Psalm 22. He will be tortured and mocked and he will be poured out like water and his heart will become like wax – and then he will lead his brothers in worship in resurrection glory (Ps 22:22). Psalm 16:10 also announces his resurrection: "You will not abandon my soul to Sheol, you will not let your Holy One see corruption."

Let's return to Peter and John and the empty tomb. John tells us the tomb was in a garden, near the place where Jesus was crucified (John 19:41). Jesus was crucified outside the garden, in the accursed place. But the tomb is in the garden. Death entered in a garden and death is now conquered in a garden.

After Peter and John find the tomb empty, they leave. Mary stays and stoops to look into the tomb and sees two angels. The empty tomb is now occupied by angels. He has conquered the grave. When Mary steps out of the empty tomb, she finds herself in the garden with someone she mistakes for the gardener. He is the gardener, indeed. The Last Adam, who is Immanuel, God with us. And he asks her a question, "Woman, why are you weeping?" (John 20:15) We can hear the echo of Isaiah 25:8: "He will swallow up death forever; and the Lord GOD will wipe away tears from all faces." This is the beginning of the end. Jesus has made atonement for sin, defeated death, and he is wiping away tears from all faces, starting with Mary.

The resurrection of Jesus is not just according to the Old Testament. He was raised according the Scriptures, both the Old and New Testaments, the prophets and the apostles. When Peter preached the Gospel of Jesus's death and resurrection to Cornelius and his household in Acts 10, he cited the testimony of history and the apostles. Cornelius and his household had heard about Jesus. They knew there was something unique about him, that he was anointed, that God was with him and was working through him. They knew about his miracles, how he healed people, and how he delivered those who were oppressed by demons. But knowing what happened is not enough. Cornelius needed to hear the testimony of the Apostle Peter:

> And we are witnesses of all that he did both in the country of the Jews and in Jerusalem. They put him to death by

> hanging him on a tree, but God raised him on the third day and made him to appear, not to all the people but to us who had been chosen by God as witnesses, who ate and drank with him after he rose from the dead. And he commanded us to preach to the people and to testify that he is the one appointed by God to be judge of the living and the dead. (Acts 10:39-42)

The apostles were chosen as witnesses to all that Jesus did, to his death, and to his resurrection. Their testimony is eyewitness testimony, but they were chosen as witness by Jesus himself and empowered by the Holy Spirit to bear witness (John 15:26-27). Their testimony is divinely appointed and empowered. The apostles did not simply testify that God was with Jesus. They bore witness to the divine identity of Jesus. In the book of Acts, Peter declares that Jesus is the Lord (2:36), the Holy and Righteous One (3:14), the Author of Life (3:15), and the Saviour (5:31). In this sermon to Cornelius, he testifies that Jesus is "Lord of all" (10:36) and "Judge of the living and the dead" (10:42).

The apostles bore witness to the identity of Jesus and to what God was doing in and through Jesus. They not only testified to what happened, but to the meaning of what happened. Yes, Jesus died on the cross and was raised on the third day, but the apostles declare that he died for our sins and that in his death, death and Satan are defeated. The apostles not only proclaimed that Jesus had died and was raised, they proclaimed that whoever believes in him receives peace and the forgiveness of sins. The apostles' Spirit-inspired and Spirit-empowered teaching is written and preserved in the New Testament and received by those who have ears to hear. Cornelius and his household had ears to hear. While Peter was still saying these things, the Holy Spirit fell on all who heard the word (Acts 10:44).

We confess that the Son of God "was raised on the third day according to the Scriptures," which are the Spirit-inspired and Spirit-illuminated witness of the Old and New Testaments to the resurrection of the Son of God.

Ascended into Heaven
Ascension follows resurrection. The Son of God, who came down from heaven, ascended into heaven. The movement of descent and ascent cannot merely be traced within spatial geography. The taunt of Russian cosmonauts that God does not exist because he could not be found beyond the earth's atmosphere only proved the error of their crude materialism. Heaven is not somewhere in outer space. God made heaven and earth, all things visible and invisible. Earth is the visible realm, which includes the heavens (sky and outer space). Heaven is the invisible realm, where heavenly creatures reside, including cherubim and seraphim who surround God's throne.

There is a veil between heaven and earth. This veil was lifted for Moses on Mount Sinai (Ex 25:40; Heb 8:5), Elijah and Elisha (1 Kgs 17:1; 2 Kgs 2:11; 6:17), Isaiah (Is 6), Ezekiel (Ezek 1-3), and John (Rev 4:1).

The Son of God, who for us men and for our salvation, came down from heaven and became man, who was crucified, suffered, and was buried, and who was raised on the third day, has ascended into heaven. As a human being, he has passed through the veil between heaven and earth. Hebrews 2 shows us the significance of his ascension by explaining the meaning of Psalm 8. In the psalm, David testifies to God concerning man:

> "You made him for a little while lower than the angels;
>   you have crowned him with glory and honour, putting everything in subjection under his feet."
> Now in putting everything in subjection to him, he left nothing outside his control. At present, we do not yet see everything in subjection to him. (Heb 2:7-8)

Even though man was created a little lower than the angels, it was God's intended end for man to crown him with glory and honour and put everything in subjection to him. But we do not see such honour or glory or subjection right now. On the contrary, not only is man a little lower than the angels, he has fallen in sin to the depths of Sheol. "But," the preacher in Hebrews continues, "we see him who for a little while was made lower than the angels, namely Jesus, crowned with glory and honour because of the suffering of death, so that by the grace of God he might taste death for everyone" (Heb 2:9). We see Jesus, the Son of God – who came down from heaven, atoned for sin, tasted death, and conquered the grave – we see him crowned with glory and honour. He ascended into heaven and he is "bringing many sons to glory" (Heb 2:10).

He is the pioneer, who, as a man, goes ahead of us into heaven. And he promises, "I will come again and will take you to myself, that where I am you may be also" (John 14:3). Thus, Leo the Great exhorted his congregation in fifth-century Rome: "Since the Ascension of Christ is our elevation, and since, where the glory of the Head has preceded us, there hope for the body is also invited, let us exult, dearly beloved, with worthy joy and be glad with a holy thanksgiving" (Sermon 73.4).[8] He ascended into heaven and he is bringing many sons to glory. Let us rejoice and give thanks!

Seated at the Right Hand of the Father
We confess the session of Christ: that Jesus Christ, the incarnate, crucified, and risen Son of God, is seated at the right hand of the Father. His session signifies his royal priestly identity and ministry.

First, his session signifies his royal identity and ministry. He is the heir of all things and upholds all things by his powerful word (Heb 1:2-3). Seated at the right hand of the Father, he is "far above all rule and authority and power and dominion, and above every name that is named, not only in this age but also in the one to come. And he put all things under his feet and gave him as head over all things to

---

8   *St. Leo the Great. Sermons*, trans. Jane Patricia Freeland and Agnes Josephine Conway, The Fathers of the Church, no. 93 (Washington, DC: The Catholic University of America Press, 1996), 324.

the church, which is his body, the fullness of him who fills all in all." (Eph 1:21-23) He sits enthroned as King of kings and Lord of lords. All authority in heaven and earth has been given to him, just as the prophets promised (Ps 110:1; Dan 7:13-14).

Second, his session signifies his priestly identity and ministry. Priestly ministry is a ministry of mediation and intercession. As a high priest, Aaron represented the people before God and he represented God before the people (Ex 28). The priests in the Old Testament never sat, they always stood. Their ministry was a standing ministry, because their work was never finished and could never be finished. Their ministry of mediation and intercession could never atone for sin and they themselves needed atonement for sin (Heb 5:1-10; 7:23-28; 9:1-10). Christ sat down at the right hand of the Father, "after making purification for sins" (Heb 1:3), having "appeared once for all at the end of the ages to put away sin by the sacrifice of himself" (Heb 9:26). He has made atonement for sin. It is finished. His work is done. He sat down.

But he has an ongoing ministry of intercession on behalf of redeemed sinners. He sits at the right hand of the Father as our representative. In fact, Paul can say that even now, God has "seated us with him in the heavenly places" (Eph 2:6) and that "our life is hidden with Christ in God" (Col 3:3). Christ is not simply our representative in heaven by name or office, but by union. We are members of his body.

As our head, seated at the right hand of the Father, he intercedes for us to the Father. His session gives us the assurance of salvation: "he holds his priesthood permanently, because he continues for ever. Consequently, he is able to save to the uttermost those who draw near to God through him, since he always lives to make intercession for them." (Heb 7:24-25)

And so, "Let us then with confidence draw near to the throne of grace, that we may receive mercy and find grace to help in time of need" (Heb 4:16). Let us "seek the things that are above, where Christ is, seated at the right hand of God" (Col 3:1). Let us bend the knee and fall down and worship: "To him who sits on the throne and to the Lamb be blessing and honour and glory and might for ever and ever!" (Rev 5:13).

He Will Come Again in Glory

We confess our faith in the second coming of Christ: "he will come again in glory." The word "glory" signifies the manifestation of God's presence. When the Son of God first came down from heaven, he came in humility, born of a peasant virgin, laid to rest in a manger. The incarnation veiled his glory, which is why the prophet declares, "he had no form of majesty that we should look at him" (Is 53:2). And yet, the incarnation manifested his glory, which is why the apostle declares, "And the Word became flesh and tabernacled among us, and we have seen his glory" – whose glory? – "glory as of the only Son from the Father, full of grace and truth" (John 1:14).

Right now, the glory of the risen Lord Jesus Christ is veiled in heaven. But Peter writes, "though you do not now see him, you believe in him and rejoice with joy that is inexpressible and filled with glory" (1 Pet 1:8). And Paul writes that when, in response to the word of the Gospel, we turn to Christ in repentance and faith, a veil is lifted: "And we all, with unveiled face, beholding the glory of the Lord, are being transformed into the same image from one degree of glory to another" (2 Cor 3:18). Even so, we behold him now by faith, but we long to see him face to face.

And we will. He will come again in glory. On that day, the veil between heaven and earth will be lifted and we will see him face to face, not by faith, but with our own (resurrected) eyes. Paul describes the second coming of Christ in 1 Thessalonians 4:16-17:

> For the Lord himself will descend from heaven with a cry of command, with the voice of an archangel, and with the sound of the trumpet of God. Then we who are alive, who are left, will be caught up together with them in the clouds to meet the Lord in the air, and so we will always be with the Lord.

The shout, the angelic voice, the sound of the trumpet, and the clouds are manifestations of God's glory (see Ex 19:16-17). What is only heard in heaven, the voice of the angel and the sound of the trumpet, is now heard on earth, because the veil between heaven and earth is lifted when Christ comes in glory.

He comes in the clouds because clouds signify both the veil between heaven and earth and the glorious presence of God. When Moses went into the cloud on Mount Sinai (Ex 24:18), he went through the veil into the very presence of God. On the Day of Atonement, the high priest entered the Holy of Holies with a censor full of burning coals and he put incense on the fire, so that when he ministered before the Ark of the Covenant, a cloud of incense would cover the mercy seat (Lev 16:2, 13). When Jesus's glory was unveiled before Peter, James, and John on the Mount of Transfiguration, a cloud descended and overshadowed them and they entered the cloud (Matt 17:5, Mark 9:7; Luke 9:17). To enter the cloud is to enter the glorious presence of God. On the last day, Christ will come in the clouds, that is, he will come again in glory. And we will see him face to face "and so we will always be with the Lord" (1 Thess 4:17).

To Judge the Living and Dead

We live east of Eden. Creation groans under the curse of the Fall, humanity is corrupted by sin, the nations and the peoples rage and plot and set themselves up against the Lord and his Anointed (Ps 2:1-2). We shine as lights in the midst of a crooked and twisted generation (Phil 2:15).

We are sometimes tempted to despair and think that sin and evil will prevail. Asaph confesses this temptation in Psalm 73. He observed the wicked and he admits:

> For I was envious of the arrogant,
>   when I saw the prosperity of the wicked.
> For they have no pangs until death;
>   their bodies are fat and sleek.

> They are not in trouble as others are;
>> they are not stricken like the rest of mankind . . .
> They scoff and speak with malice;
>> loftily they threaten oppression.
> They set their mouths against the heavens,
>> and their tongue struts through the earth . . .
> And they say, "How can God know?
>> Is there knowledge in the Most High?"
> Behold, these are the wicked;
>> always at ease, they increase in riches . . .
> But when I thought how to understand this,
>> it seemed to me a wearisome task,
> until I went into the sanctuary of God;
>> then I discerned their end. (Ps 73:3-5, 8-9, 11-12, 16-17)

Trying to reckon with sin and evil and the apparent success of the wicked will wear you out. Asaph needed to view the current state of the world from the sanctuary, in the light of the end. We reckon with the sin and evil in the world knowing that Christ "will come again in glory to judge the living and the dead."

The apostles proclaimed this end-time perspective when they preached the Gospel. Peter testified to Cornelius and his household: "[Christ] commanded us to preach to the people and to testify that he is the one appointed by God to be judge of the living and the dead" (Acts 10:42). This Gospel testimony comes from Jesus himself, who testifies that the Father "has given him authority to execute judgement, because he is the Son of Man" (John 5:27; cf. Dan 7:9-14).

It's Good News that Jesus will come again to judge the living and dead. Consider the following question and answer in the Heidelberg Catechism:

> Question 52: How does Christ's return "to judge the living and the dead" comfort you?
>> Answer: In all distress and persecution, with uplifted

head I confidently await the very judge who has already offered himself to the judgment of God in my place and removed the whole curse from me. Christ will cast all his enemies and mine into everlasting condemnation, but will take me and all his chosen ones to himself into the joy and glory of heaven.[9]

In the trials and tribulations of this life, when we grieve and groan because of the sin and evil in this world, we remember that our Saviour will come again to the judge the living and the dead. On that day, we will be vindicated in him. On that day, he will vanquish and destroy once for all those who rage and plot against him and the Church. And on that day, he will take us to himself and we will hear a loud voice from the throne saying,

> Behold, the dwelling place of God is with man. He will dwell with them, and they will be his people, and God himself will be with them as their God. He will wipe away every tear from their eyes, and death shall be no more, neither shall there be mourning, nor crying, nor pain any more, for the former things have passed away. (Rev 21:3-4)

And His Kingdom Will Have No End

God made Adam and Eve in his image and blessed them and commanded them to subdue the earth and have dominion. As the image of God, we are called to rule in a way that reflects God's justice, holiness, mercy, and love; however, because we exchanged the truth of God for the serpent's lie, our rule reflects the creature, rather than the Creator. Our rule is beastly. In Daniel 7, the prophet reports what he saw in visions by night: "four great beasts came up out of the sea" (Dan 7:3). The beasts represent kings and kingdoms, which characterize the beastly kingdoms of the earth through the ages.

---

[9] *The Heidelberg Catechism*, 29.

But that is not all Daniel sees:

> I saw in the night visions, and behold, with the clouds of heaven there came one like a son of man, and he came to the Ancient of Days and was presented before him. And to him was given dominion and glory and a kingdom, that all peoples, nations, and languages should serve him; his dominion is an everlasting dominion, which shall not pass away, and his kingdom one that shall not be destroyed. (Dan 7:13-14)

Daniel sees a vision of the Son of Man, a truly human king, who will conquer and judge the beastly kingdoms. His kingdom rule and reign are eternal and all peoples, nations, and languages will serve him. As God promised concerning this king through the prophet Isaiah:

> Of the increase of his government and of peace
>   there will be no end,
> on the throne of David and over his kingdom,
>   to establish it and to uphold it
> with justice and with righteousness
>   from this time forth and for evermore. (Is 9:7)

Jesus is the king Isaiah promised and Daniel saw in his night visions. The angel Gabriel announced to Mary:

> And behold, you will conceive in your womb and bear a son, and you shall call his name Jesus. He will be great and will be called the Son of the Most High. And the Lord God will give to him the throne of his father David, and he will reign over the house of Jacob for ever, and of his kingdom there will be no end. (Luke 1:31-33)

We confess the eternal rule and reign of Christ. What Daniel saw in his night vision came to pass when Jesus ascended on the clouds into heaven. The Lord Jesus Christ is the Son of Man who is now seated at the right hand of the Father and he is now subduing all his enemies (Ps 110:1; 1 Cor 15:27-28; Heb 1:10, 13). He is "the ruler of the kings on earth" (Rev 1:5) and "the King of kings" (1 Tim 6:15; Rev 19:16). The beastly kingdoms of this earth remain, but we know their days are numbered, for "he will come again in glory to judge the living and the dead, and his kingdom will have no end." And he has made us a kingdom and priests and we shall reign on the earth (Rev 5:10; 2 Tim 2:12). "Therefore," the book of Hebrews exhorts, "let us be grateful for receiving a kingdom that cannot be shaken, and thus let us offer to God acceptable worship, with reverence and awe" (Heb 12:28).

4
We Believe in the Holy Spirit

We believe in the Holy Spirit, the Lord, the Giver of Life, who proceeds from the Father [and the Son]. With the Father and the Son he is worshipped and glorified. He has spoken through the Prophets. We believe in one holy, catholic, and apostolic Church. We confess one baptism for the forgiveness of sins. And we look for the resurrection of the dead and the life of the world to come. Amen.

The Nicene Creed has three paragraphs in which we confess our faith in the Triune God: Father, Son, and Holy Spirit. The original creed drafted at the Council of Nicaea in 325 only had one line on the Holy Spirit, simply confessing: "We believe in the Holy Spirit." In the decades following the Council of Nicaea, the Church was confronted with various teachers who denied the divinity of the Spirit, just as the Arians denied the divinity of the Son.

Athanasius of Alexandria (ca.296/98–373) defended the divinity of the Holy Spirit from Scripture, just as he had defended the divinity of the Son from Scripture:

> We still need to examine, one by one, each passage in the Divine Scriptures that speaks about the Holy Spirit. Like good bankers, we need to judge whether the Spirit has anything that is proper to creatures or whether he is proper to God. In this manner we will be able to determine whether to call him a creature or something other than creatures and proper to and one of the divinity of the Trinity. (*Ep. Serap.* I.21.4)[1]

Athanasius goes on to demonstrate from Scripture that the Holy Spirit is God.

Basil of Caesarea (330–379) and Gregory of Nazianzus (329–390) also defended the divinity of the Holy Spirit, drawing out the implications of a right doctrine of the Holy Spirit for a right doctrine of God, creation, salvation, Scripture, the Christian life, the Church, and worship. For example, Basil warns us:

> If someone rejects the Spirit, his faith in the Father and the Son is made useless; it is impossible to believe in the Father and the Son without the presence of the Spirit. He who rejects the Spirit rejects the Son, and he who rejects the Son rejects the Father. "No one can say 'Jesus is Lord' except in the Holy Spirit" (1 Cor 12:3), and "no one has ever seen God; the only begotten, who is in the bosom of the Father, He has made him known" (John 1:18). Such a person has no part in true worship. It is impossible to worship the Son except in the Holy Spirit; it is impossible to call upon the Father except in the Spirit of adoption. (*On the Holy Spirit* 11.27)[2]

When the Council of Constantinople met in 381, one of the issues

---

1 *Works on the Spirit*, trans. DelCogliano, Radde-Gallwitz, and Ayres, 86.
2 *On the Holy Spirit*, Ttrans. Anderson, 48.

they addressed was the doctrine of the Holy Spirit. They recognized that the Church cannot simply confess that we believe in the Holy Spirit, so they elaborated the Creed's third paragraph:

> We believe in the Holy Spirit, the Lord, the Giver of Life, who proceeds from the Father [and the Son]. With the Father and the Son he is worshipped and glorified. He has spoken through the Prophets.

The Holy Spirit is the Lord, which means he is Yahweh, I AM. He is the Giver of Life, both in creation and redemption. He proceeds from the Father [and the Son]. (See below why the Eastern and Western Christians disagree on this point.) He is worshipped and glorified with the Father and the Son, which means our worship must be robustly trinitarian. He has spoken through the prophets, which means the Scriptures are Spirit-inspired and Spirit-illuminated, Spirit-given and Spirit-received.

We Believe in the Holy Spirit, the Lord
We confess that "we believe in one Lord, Jesus Christ" and we confess that "we believe in the Holy Spirit, the Lord." Lord (*Kurios* in Greek) refers to the divine name, Yahweh. Israel is summoned in Deuteronomy 6:4-5: "Hear, O Israel: The LORD our God, the LORD is one. You shall love the LORD your God with all your heart and with all your soul and with all your might." Israel's confession of faith in Yahweh is trinitarian. The one LORD, Yahweh, is Father, Son, and Holy Spirit.

In the late fourth century, when many Christians questioned whether the Holy Spirit is God, Gregory of Nazianzus preached a sermon defending the divinity of the Spirit. Some argued the divinity of the Spirit is not in the Bible. Gregory responded: "But now you shall have a swarm of proof-texts, from which the Godhead of the Holy Spirit can be proved thoroughly scriptural" (*Oration* 31.29).[3]

---

3 Trans. Wickham, *On God and Christ*, 139.

Among the swarm of scriptural texts to which Gregory alludes are several texts from 1 and 2 Corinthians:[4]

> For the Spirit searches everything, even the depths of God. For who knows a person's thoughts except the spirit of that person, which is in him? So also no one comprehends the thoughts of God except the Spirit of God. (1 Cor 2:10-11)

Only I know my own thoughts. Only you know your own thoughts. Only God knows his own thoughts. If the Spirit of God knows the thoughts of God, he must be God.

> But you were washed, you were sanctified, you were justified in the name of the Lord Jesus Christ and by the Spirit of our God. (1 Cor 6:11)

Only God, who is holy, can sanctify. He is the source and subject of sanctification, but never the object. He sanctifies; his creatures are sanctified. If we are sanctified by the Holy Spirit, he must be God.

> But when one turns to the Lord, the veil is removed. Now the Lord is the Spirit, and where the Spirit of the Lord is, there is freedom. And we all, with unveiled face, beholding the glory of the Lord, are being transformed into the same image from one degree of glory to another. For this comes from the Lord who is the Spirit. (2 Cor 3:16-18)

Here Paul explicitly writes that the Holy Spirit is the Lord. He also assumes that the Lord is triune. We turn to the Lord (the Father) in repentance, we behold the glory of the Lord (the Son), and we are

---

4   *Oration* 31.29, trans. Wickham, *On God and Christ*, 139-140. Cf. Michael Haykin, *The Spirit of God: The Exegesis of 1 and 2 Corinthians in the Pneumatomachian Controversy of the Fourth Century*, Supplements to Vigiliae Christianae, no.27 (Leiden: E. J. Brill, 1994).

transformed from one degree of glory to another by the Lord who is the Spirit.

> The grace of the Lord Jesus Christ and the love of God and the fellowship of the Holy Spirit be with you all. (2 Cor 13:14)

Paul's benediction is thoroughly trinitarian. We know the grace of the Lord Jesus Christ and the love of God the Father by our fellowship with the Spirit. To be in communion with the Spirit is to be in communion with God, because the Spirit is God.

The Giver of Life

The Holy Spirit is the Giver of Life. We see the Spirit's life-giving work in Genesis 1:2: "The earth was without form and void, and darkness was over the face of the deep. And the Spirit of God was hovering over the face of the waters. And God said …" Creation begins with the Spirit of God and the Word of God. When the earth was without form and void, the hovering Spirit of God formed and filled according to the Word of God.

The life-giving work of the Spirit in creation is commemorated in Psalm 104:30:

> When you send forth your Spirit, they are created,
>   and you renew the face of the ground.

The life-giving Spirit of God is the renewing Spirit. Ezekiel records a vision of the Spirit's life-giving renewal in Ezekiel 47. The prophet sees a river flowing east from the temple, through the desert of the Araba, into the Dead Sea. Ezekiel hears the Word of the Lord: "And wherever the river goes, every living creature that swarms will live, and there will be very many fish. For this water goes there, that the waters of the sea may become fresh; so everything will live where the river goes" (Ezek 47:9).

The river in Ezekiel's vision is the river from Eden, which watered the garden and separated into four rivers to water and give life to the whole world (Gen 2:10). John sees the same river – "the river of the water of life" – in his vision of the new creation (Rev 22:1). When our Lord alludes to Ezekiel's vision in John 7, he makes it clear that the river, the water of life, is the Holy Spirit. The Spirit is the living water, the Giver of Life.

The Spirit is the Giver of Life to the believer. In Ezekiel 36, God promises that he will cleanse us with water, he will remove our heart of stone and give us a heart of flesh, and he will put his Spirit within us (Ezek 36:25-27). In the next chapter, the same Spirit is breathed over a valley of dry bones, which are resurrected and filled with the Spirit (Ezek 37:1-14). The Lord Jesus announced the fulfillment of Ezekiel's prophecy when he told Nicodemus that he must be born again, that is, born of the Spirit (John 3:1-8).

The Spirit is the Giver of Life in creation and redemption. He gives life to the dead. On the first day of the week, when darkness was over the face of the deep, the Spirit hovered over the face of waters (Gen 1:2). On the first of the week, while it was still dark, Mary Magdalene found the tomb empty. The Spirit, the Giver of Life, gave life to the crucified Saviour: "If the Spirit of him who raised Jesus from the dead dwells in you, he who raised Christ Jesus from the dead will also give life to your mortal bodies through his Spirit who dwells in you" (Rom 8:11).

Who Proceeds from the Father

We confess that the Holy Spirit proceeds from the Father. With this statement we are confessing a truth about the identity of God. Gregory of Nazianzus insisted we look to Scripture alone for the doctrine of God. We cannot say more or less about God than Scripture reveals. Looking to Scripture, Gregory notes that the names Father, Son, and Spirit are tied to their relationship with one another and the manner in which the Son and the Spirit have their being from the Father. The Son and Spirit are what the Father is, because they are from the Father.

The unity and oneness of God has its source in the Father's being, which he shares with the Son and the Spirit. Scripture reveals that the Son is "the only-begotten from the Father" (John 1:14) and the Spirit "proceeds from the Father" (John 15:26). The Spirit is the Spirit because he proceeds from the Father. The Son is the Son because he is begotten from the Father. The Father is the Father because he has begotten the Son.

The Father is unbegotten, the Son is begotten, and the Spirit proceeds. The terms unbegotten, begotten, and procession are not definitive of God's divine being; rather, they signify three properties, which distinguish the three persons and their relationship to one another as Father, Son, and Spirit. When we are thinking about the triune God, we must remember that God is eternal. To say that the Son and Spirit have their being *from* the Father does not mean they have their being *after* the Father. The Father has always been the Father; the Son has always been the Son; and the Spirit has always been the Spirit.

We may wonder how the Son is begotten from the Father and how the Spirit proceeds from the Father? Gregory writes that such a question "ought to have the tribute of our reverent silence" (*Oration* 29.8).[5] Scripture reveals *that* the Son is begotten from the Father and the Spirit proceeds from the Father. Scripture does not explain *how* the Son is begotten and the Spirit proceeds. Such knowledge belongs to God and we dare not pry into such a divine mystery (*Oration* 31.8). Reverent silence is the fitting response.

[And the Son]

The Western, Latin text of the Nicene Creed has an extra word after "from the Father": *filioque* which translated means "and the Son." Why this addition and what difference does it make whether we confess that the Holy Spirit proceeds from the Father or from the Father and the Son?

To begin, let us not dismiss this as a silly controversy in history

---

5 *On God and Christ*, trans. Wickham, 76.

that does not really matter for us. Our confession of who God is, as he has made himself known through Scripture, really does matter. God is who he is. If we are not surrendered to his self-revelation, we are making God who we want him to be and that is idolatry. We call right theology orthodoxy (right doxology) because it gives us the language of true and faithful worship. Our confession that the Holy Spirit proceeds from the Father cites the words of Jesus himself in John 15:26 and reveals something very important about the triune God. God is one because he is one in being. The Spirit and Son have their being from the Father and they are one in being with the Father. The Son is eternally begotten from the Father and the Spirit eternally proceeds from the Father. Begetting and proceeding distinguishes Father, Son, and Spirit: the Trinity.

The word *filioque* ("and the Son") was added to the Creed by a council of Western bishops in Toledo in 589. The Church in Spain was still fighting Arianism, a heresy that denied the divinity of the Son and the Son's unity in being with the Father. By saying that the Spirit proceeds from the Father and the Son, the council was trying to say that the Father and the Son are one in being. This addition was not widely accepted among Western churches. In the early 800s, the Emperor Charlemagne promoted the addition, but Pope Leo III opposed it. It was not adopted in Rome until the year 1014, when the Holy Roman Emperor Henry II wanted the *filioque* added to the Creed at his coronation mass.

The year 1054 marks the official schism between the Eastern (Orthodox) and Western (Roman Catholic) churches. The addition of *filioque* ("and the Son") in the Creed was one of the reasons the Eastern and Western churches split. A proper history of this schism must consider various political, cultural, ecclesiastical, and theological factors; however, the *filioque* was a major theological factor.

The Western position is well articulated by Augustine, Anselm, and Aquinas. Here is my very cursory (and partial) presentation of what they say: The Son has his being from the Father. He is the Son because he is begotten from the Father. The Father is the Father because he begets the Son. We cannot say that the Son has his being from the Father and the Spirit, because that would make the Spirit the Father of the Son, which is absurd. We can say, however, that the Spirit proceeds from the Son, without contradicting the unique identity of the Son or the Spirit. Augustine argues that the Father and Son are a single source of the Spirit, who proceeds from the unity of the Father and the Son. The Son himself has his being from the Father and the Spirit has his being from the Father and the Son.

That the Spirit proceeds from the Father and the Son is suggested by Paul's declaration in Galatians 4:6: "God has sent the Spirit of his Son into our hearts, crying 'Abba! Father!'" The Spirit is the Spirit of Adoption because he proceeds from the Father and the Son and by virtue of the Father sending the Spirit of his Son into our hearts, we cry out, "Abba! Father!" Finally, it is often argued in the West that because we read that the Son sends the Spirit (John 15:26) and breathes the Spirit (John 20:22), we may also infer that the Spirit proceeds from the Son.

Theologians from the East have typically responded to the above presentation by noting the distinction between the being or essence of the triune God and the activity or operation of the triune God. Put simply, we need to recognize the difference between who God is and what God does. The question of the Spirit's procession is a question about who God is. He is Father, Son, and Holy Spirit because the Son is begotten from the Father and the Spirit proceeds from the Father. The sending of the Spirit is not a question of who God is but what God does. The Father sends the Son, who then sends the Spirit. The Spirit glorifies the Son, just as the Son glorifies the Father. Sending and glorifying refer to the activity of the triune God, not the being of the triune God.

In my view, I think it is important to consider the distinction between the being of God and the activity of God. The East is right to distinguish procession and sending. Eastern theologians also question Augustine's view that the Father and the Son are a single source of the Spirit, because it implies the Father and the Son are one person, which is a heresy known as Sebellianism or modalism.

In the end, I am left pondering Galatians 4:6: "God has sent the Spirit of his Son into our hearts, crying 'Abba! Father!'" Whatever our views on how to understand the procession of the Holy Spirit, I can only marvel and praise God for such grace: the Father has sent the Spirit of his Son into our hearts, crying "Abba! Father!" Whoa! Hallelujah! And this is where the Creed leads us, for the very next phrase is, "who is worshipped and glorified with the Father and the Son." Yes! Glory be to God the Father, God the Son, and God the Holy Spirit!

With the Father and the Son He Is Worshipped and Glorified

Our liturgy reveals our theology. The Nicene Creed reminds us that we worship and glorify the Triune God: Father, Son, and Holy Spirit. That is why we confess concerning the Holy Spirit: "with the Father and the Son he is worshipped and glorified." This statement recognizes and affirms the inherent trinitarian expression of biblical doxology and benediction. For example, when the Apostle Paul blesses God, he blesses the Father, Son, and Holy Spirit (Eph 1:3-14) and when he blesses believers, his benediction is trinitarian: "May the grace of the Lord Jesus Christ and the love of God and the fellowship of the Holy Spirit be with you all" (2 Cor 13:14). Likewise, when the Apostle John extends grace to his readers, the source of his benediction is the Triune God: "Grace to you and peace from him who is and was and is to come, and from the seven spirits who are before this throne, and from Jesus Christ the faithful witness, the firstborn of the dead, and the ruler of kings on earth" (Rev 1:4b-5a). (The sevenfold spirit is the Holy Spirit.)

Following the biblical pattern, our language of prayer, praise, doxology, and benediction is trinitarian. Here we see a relationship between doctrine and worship, liturgy and creed. Right theology and right worship go together. Orthodoxy can be translated "right opinion or thought," but it can also be translated "right worship." Gregory of Nazianzus reminds us that right worship is the end of right doctrine. He puts it succinctly in one of his theological poems: "The sum of the matter is this: worship the Trinity" (*Poem* 1.1.10, 74).[6] For Gregory, right theology and right worship motivates mission. He concludes a series of sermons on the Trinity: "To the best of my powers I will persuade all men to worship Father, Son, and Holy Spirit as the single Godhead and power, because to him belong all glory, honor, and might for ever and ever" (*Oration* 31.33).[7]

With the Psalmist we cry out: "Let the peoples praise you, O God; let all the peoples praise you!" (Ps 67:3,5). With the apostles and the Church through the centuries, we call on the nations to worship and glorify the Triune God: Father, Son, and Spirit.

He Has Spoken through the Prophets
This is a statement about the Holy Spirit and Holy Scripture. That the Spirit speaks through the Scriptures is the testimony of the Scriptures themselves. In Acts 1:16, Peter addresses the gathered believers in Jerusalem concerning the treachery and death of Judas: "Brothers, the Scripture had to be fulfilled, which the Holy Spirit spoke beforehand by the mouth of David . . ." The Holy Spirit spoke through David and David himself knew it. He testifies at the end of his life: "the Spirit of the LORD speaks by me; his word is on my tongue" (2 Sam 23:2). The Apostle Paul gives the same testimony as David: "And we impart this in words not taught by human wisdom but taught by the Spirit" (1 Cor 2:13). Like David, Paul was aware that his words were Spirit-given. In fact, he writes Timothy that "all Scripture is breathed out by God" (2 Tim 3:16). For this reason, because the Bible is Spirit-given, it is perfect, reviving the soul; it is sure, making wise the simple; it is right, rejoicing the heart; it is pure, enlightening the eyes; it is true and righteous altogether (Ps 19:7-9).

The ministry of the Spirit, speaking through the Scriptures, makes the Bible a living and active word. Thus, when the author of Hebrews

---

6 *On God and Man: The Theological Poetry of St Gregory of Nazianzus*, trans. Peter Gilbert, (Crestwood, NY: SVS Press, 2001), 83.

7 *On God and Christ*, trans. Wickham, 143.

quotes Psalm 95, he introduces the quotation with these words: "Therefore, as the Holy Spirit says, 'Today, if you hear his voice . . .'" (Heb 3:7). When the Word of God is read and heard, the Spirit of God is speaking. But not everyone has ears to hear. When the risen Lord Jesus addresses the seven churches in Revelation 2-3, he exhorts each church: "He who has an ear, let him hear what the Spirit says to the churches" (Rev 2:7, 11, 17, 29; 3:6, 13, 22). The Spirit speaks through the Scriptures, but the Spirit must also give us ears to hear. Paul warns us, "The natural person does not accept the things of the Spirit of God, for they are folly to him, and he is not able to understand them because they are spiritually discerned" (1 Cor 2:14).

What do those with ears to hear, hear? We hear the voice of the Son. The Spirit bears witness to the Son (John 15:26), so that we may recognize him, hear his call, and turn to him in repentance and faith. We are like sheep who recognize and follow the voice of our Shepherd. As Jesus says concerning his sheep, "A stranger they will not follow, but they will flee from him, for they do not know the voice of strangers" (John 10:5) There are many voices speaking to us through media and social media. But we do not listen to the voice of strangers. We listen to the voice of the Good Shepherd: "My sheep hear my voice, and I know them, and they follow me" (John 10:27). By the Spirit we hear his voice in the Scriptures.

This truth has practical consequences. He has spoken through the prophets, not through the podcasts. How do we know his voice if we so rarely hear it. Let us take up the Scriptures and let us read and hear and heed the Word of the Lord.

We Believe in One, Holy, Catholic, and Apostolic Church

In the second paragraph of the Nicene Creed, we confess our faith in the Son of God and his saving work. In the third paragraph, we confess our faith in the Holy Spirit and his ministry. When we confess that "we believe in one, holy, catholic, and apostolic Church," we are confessing something about the ministry of the Spirit in the Church. It is by the Holy Spirit that the Church is one, holy, catholic, and apostolic.

The Church is one. We are the one body and bride of Christ, "for in one Spirit we were all baptized into one body—Jews or Greeks, slaves or free" (1 Cor 12:13). We must be "eager to maintain the unity of the Spirit in the bond of peace," because "there is one body and one Spirit" (Eph 4:3-4).

The Church is holy because we are anointed, filled, and sealed with the Holy Spirit: "Do you not know that you are God's temple and that God's Spirit dwells in you? If anyone destroys God's temple, God will destroy him. For God's temple is holy, and you are that temple" (1 Cor 3:16-17).

The Church is catholic. The one body of Christ comprises many members, "from every nation, from all tribes and peoples and languages" (Rev 7:9). The catholicity of the Church is manifest in the gift of the Spirit to the nations. As the Apostle Peter testified to the council in Jerusalem: "Brothers, you know that in the early days God made a choice among you, that by my mouth the Gentiles should hear the word of the gospel and believe. And God, who knows the heart, bore witness to them, by giving them the Holy Spirit just as he did to us, and he made no distinction between us and them, having cleansed their hearts by faith." (Acts 15:7-9)

Finally, the Church is apostolic. Jesus said to his disciples at the Last Supper: "But when the Helper comes, whom I will send to you from the Father, the Spirit of truth, who proceeds from the Father, he will bear witness about me. And you also will bear witness, because you have been with me from the beginning." (John 15:26-27) The Spirit's witness to the Son is communicated through the apostolic witness. The Church is planted and nourished by the Gospel witness of Jesus's Spirit-empowered apostles.

By the Holy Spirit, the Church is one, holy, catholic, and apostolic.

The Church is One

The Church is the one body and bride of Christ, "for in one Spirit we were all baptized into one body—Jews or Greeks, slaves or free" (1

Cor 12:13). The Church is one because the Father, Son, and Spirit are one. The one Church has one faith in the one God. As Paul writes in Ephesians 4:4-6: "There is one body and one Spirit—just as you were called to the one hope that belongs to your call—one Lord, one faith, one baptism, one God and Father of all, who is over all and through all and in all." We are one and we must guard our unity and grow in unity. We must be "eager to maintain the unity of the Spirit in the bond of peace" (Eph 4:3) and we must "build up the body of Christ until we attain the unity of faith" and "the measure of the stature of the fullness of Christ" (Eph 4:12-13).

It is the ministry of the saints, the ministry of every member of the Church, that promotes this growth towards greater unity and maturity in Christ. Christ has given apostles, prophets, evangelists, shepherds, and teachers to equip the saints for the work of ministry. Various aspects of the saints' ministry are outlined in passages like Romans 12, Ephesians 5-6, Colossians 3, Titus 2, etc. As we are gifted and equipped by the Spirit of God for ministry, we must also be engaged in ministry. We cannot be disconnected or disengaged from the body of Christ. On the contrary, Paul exhorts us: "speaking the truth in love, we are to grow up in every way into him who is the head, into Christ, from whom the whole body, joined and held together by every joint with which it is equipped, when each part is working properly, makes the body grow so that it builds itself up in love" (Eph 4:15-16).

Paul warns that if we are disconnected and disengaged, if we are virtually connected to our screens rather than vitally connected to the one body of Christ, then we will be "tossed to and fro by the waves and carried about by every wind of doctrine, by human cunning, by craftiness in deceitful schemes" (Eph 4:14).

Finally, the unity of the Church not only sustains and promotes our maturity in Christ, it sustains and promotes our witness to Christ. Our Lord prayed for the Church and all those who would believe in him, "that they may all be one, just as you, Father, are in me, and I in you, that they also may be in us, so that the world may believe that you have sent me" (John 17:21).

The Church Is Holy

The Church is holy because by the Spirit we are set apart as holy through Christ, we are being made holy in Christ, and we will be presented holy to Christ on the last day.

First, the Church is holy because by the Spirit, we are set apart as holy unto God through the death of Christ for us: "we have been sanctified through the offering of the body of Jesus Christ once for all" (Heb 10:10). Thus, Paul opens his letter to the Corinthians: "To the church of God that is in Corinth, to those sanctified in Christ Jesus, called to be saints together with all those who in every place call upon the name of our Lord Jesus Christ" (1 Cor 10:2). This consecration as saints or holy ones, is confirmed by the seal of the Holy Spirit, who dwells in us: "Do you not know that you are God's temple and that God's Spirit dwells in you? If anyone destroys God's temple, God will destroy him. For God's temple is holy, and you are that temple" (1 Cor 3:16-17). Yes, you may have been sexually immoral, idolaters, adulterers, practising homosexuality, greedy, drunkards, revilers, and swindlers, "but you were washed, you were sanctified, you were justified in the name of the Lord Jesus Christ and by the Spirit of our God" (1 Cor 6:9-11).

Second, the Church is holy because by the Spirit, we are being sanctified in Christ. We are becoming more and more holy: "For this is the will of God, your sanctification: that you abstain from sexual immorality; that each one of you know how to control his own body in holiness and honour . . . For God has not called us for impurity, but in holiness" (1 Thess 4:3-4,7). Having been sanctified, we renounce impurity and pursue holiness. Sanctification is not abstract or theoretical. No, we present our bodies as "a living sacrifice, holy and acceptable to God" (Rom 12:1). If we turn from presenting ourselves to God and present ourselves to impurity, the Lord who has sanctified us, will discipline us: "he disciplines us for our good, that we may share his holiness" (Heb 12:10).

By the Spirit, we are set apart as holy through Christ, we are being made holy in Christ, and, finally, we will be presented holy to Christ on the last day. Our Lord will complete the good work he has begun in us (Phil 1:6). The same Lord Jesus who loved us and gave his life for us, cleanses us with the word, "so that he might present the church to himself in splendour, without spot or wrinkle or any such thing, that she might be holy and without blemish" (Eph 5:25-27). John saw a vision of the Church on the last day, "clothed with fine linen, bright and pure" (Rev 19:8). For this reason, Paul could pronounce this benediction to the church in Thessalonica: "Now may the God of peace himself sanctify you completely, and may your whole spirit and soul and body be kept blameless at the coming of our Lord Jesus Christ. He who calls you is faithful; he will surely do it." (1 Thess 5:23-24). Yes! He will surely do it!

The Church is Catholic

Evangelical Protestants may feel uncomfortable with the term "catholic" because of its connotation with Roman Catholicism. If we confess that the Church is catholic, do we imply a necessary allegiance to the Roman Catholic church and everything it represents? Some churches have updated the Creed by replacing the word "catholic" with "Christian;" however, I would argue we do not need to update the wording, we need to retrieve the meaning. The word "catholic" carries the idea of wholeness. To say the Church is catholic is to say something about its wholeness, its breadth and depth. Here's what Cyril of Jerusalem, a pastor in the 4th century, says about the catholicity of the Church in his *Catechetical Lectures*:

> The church is called catholic then because it extends over all the world, from one end of the earth to the other; and because it teaches universally and completely one and all the doctrines which ought to come to men's knowledge, concerning things both visible and invisible, heavenly and earthly; and because it brings into subjection to godliness the whole race of mankind, governors and governed, learned and unlearned; and because it universally treats

and heals the whole class of sins, which are committed by soul or body, and possesses in itself every form of virtue which is named, both in deeds and words, and in every kind of spiritual gift. (*Catech.* 18.23)[8]

That's a long sentence. Cyril gives four reasons why the Church is catholic.

First, the Church is catholic "because it extends over all the world." The Church is global. It includes people from every tribe, nation, and language (Rom 7:9). Linguistic and ethnic diversity are a mark of the Church (Eph 3:10).

Second, the Church is catholic "because it teaches universally and completely one and all the doctrines which ought to come to men's knowledge." The Church both preserves and promotes the whole counsel of God, without addition or subtraction (Acts 20:27; 2 Tim 3:16-17). The Church is catholic because it preaches and teaches the Scriptures, the whole counsel of God.

Third, the Church is catholic "because it brings into subjection to godliness the whole race of mankind, governors and governed, learned and unlearned." People from every walk of life are brought to repentance and grow in godliness in the Church. The Church is no respecter of persons. Its community compromises men and women from every socio-economic background (Gal 3:27; Col 3:11; 1 Cor 1:26).

Fourth, the Church is catholic "because it universally treats and heals the whole class of sins, which are committed by soul or body, and possesses in itself every form of virtue which is named, both in deeds and words, and in every kind of spiritual gift." The whole counsel of God is not only taught, but applied to the whole person and every aspect of life. To be catholic is to be obedient to the whole counsel of God. To be catholic is to be wholly submitted to our Lord

---

8 Cyril of Jerusalem, *Gregory Nazianzen*, trans. Edmond Hamilton Gifford, Nicene and Post-Nicene Fathers, Second Series, No.7 (Grand Rapids, MI: Eerdmans, 1976), 139-140.

Jesus Christ and wholly committed to his service.

The Church is catholic because it is global and compromises people from every walk of life who are wholly submitted to the whole counsel of God, wholly serving and growing in Christ.

The Church is Apostolic
The first generation of believers who received the Word of God from the apostles on the day of Pentecost devoted themselves to the Apostles' teaching (Acts 2:42). The Apostle Paul testifies, "I did not shrink from declaring to you the whole counsel of God" (Acts 20:27). The Church is apostolic because it is devoted to the Apostles' teaching, that is, the whole counsel God, preserved in the Bible.

Devotion to the Apostles' teaching requires faithfully receiving, guarding, and passing on God's Word. This process of receiving, guarding, and passing on was initiated and mandated by the apostles themselves. The Apostle Paul charged Timothy, "by the Holy Spirit who dwells in you, guard the good deposit entrusted to you" (2 Tim 1:14) and "what you have heard from me in the presence of many witnesses entrust to faithful men, who will be able to teach others also" (2 Tim 2:2). The good deposit passes through four generations in these verses, from Paul to Timothy to faithful men to those instructed by faithful men, and it continued to be passed on until now. When we confess the Church is apostolic, we are saying that the church receives, guards, and passes on the faith once for all delivered to the saints (Jude 1:3).

The process of receiving, guarding, and passing on the faith is not haphazard, but institutional. In every church, the apostles appointed elders (Acts 14:23) who bear the responsibility of "entrusting faithful men who will be able to teach others also" (2 Tim 2:2). We live in an age when it is all too easy to accumulate online teachers to suit our own passions and soothe our itching ears. We do not belong to the one, holy, catholic, and apostolic church by subscribing to a YouTube channel or podcast. We belong to the apostolic church by committing to a local church and submitting to elders who faithfully minister God's Word.

Finally, let us remember that when we confess the Church is apostolic, we are saying something about the presence and ministry of the Holy Spirit. It was the Spirit-filled community of believers that devoted themselves to the apostles' teaching in Acts 2. It is "by the Holy Spirit who dwells in you" that Timothy received and guarded and passed on the good deposit entrusted to him. Our identity as the apostolic Church is a sign of the Spirit's empowering presence.

We Confess One Baptism for the Forgiveness of Sins
We confess one baptism because, "there is one body and one Spirit—just as you were called to the one hope that belongs to your call— one Lord, one faith, one baptism, one God and Father of all, who is over all and through all and in all" (Eph 4:4-6). Our one baptism belongs to the unity of the Spirit and the body of Christ, and the unity of our hope and faith in one God and one Lord. For this reason, if you have been baptized into the one body of Christ, you do not need to be "re-baptized" when you join a new local church or when you have left the Church for a time and returned. We confess one baptism in the name of the Father, Son, and Holy Spirit.

We confess one baptism for the forgiveness of sins. Does this mean the rite of baptism itself forgives our sins? No. The Creed is citing Peter's response to those who heard and believed the Gospel in Acts 2:37-38:

> Now when they heard this they were cut to the heart, and said to Peter and the rest of the apostles, "Brothers, what shall we do?" And Peter said to them, "Repent and be baptized every one of you in the name of Jesus Christ for the forgiveness of your sins, and you will receive the gift of the Holy Spirit."

Paul explains the relationship between baptism, faith, and the forgiveness of sins. First, he writes in Romans 4:11: "[Abraham] received the sign of circumcision as a seal of the righteousness that he had by faith while he was still uncircumcised." Circumcision was a sign and seal of the righteousness Abraham had by faith. Paul elaborates in Colossians 2:11-14, where he writes that just as circumcision was a sign and seal of righteousness by faith, so now, in the new covenant, baptism is a sign and seal of righteousness by faith:

> In him also you were circumcised with a circumcision made without hands, by putting off the body of the flesh, by the circumcision of Christ, having been buried with him in baptism, in which you were also raised with him through faith in the powerful working of God, who raised him from the dead. And you, who were dead in your trespasses and the uncircumcision of your flesh, God made alive together with him, having forgiven us all our trespasses, by cancelling the record of debt that stood against us with its legal demands. This he set aside, nailing it to the cross.

This is why we confess one baptism for the forgiveness of sins, because baptism is a sign and seal that when we were dead in our trespasses and the uncircumcision of our flesh, God made us alive together with Christ, having forgiven us all our trespasses. For this reason — because God made us alive together with Christ — Paul exhorts us,

> So you also must consider yourselves dead to sin and alive to God in Christ Jesus. Let not sin therefore reign in your mortal body, to make you obey its passions. Do not present your members to sin as instruments for unrighteousness, but present yourselves to God as those who have been brought from death to life, and your members to God as instruments for righteousness. For sin will have no dominion over you, since you are not under law but under grace. (Rom 6:11-14)

We Look for the Resurrection of the Dead

The Nicene Creed ends in hope, orienting us to the resurrection of the dead and the life of the world to come. God's Word affirms the goodness of the material creation from the divine inspection of creation in Genesis 1, "and God saw that it was good," to the new creation in Revelation 21-22, "adorned as a bride for her husband." Between creation and new creation is the climax of history: the incarnation, death, resurrection, and ascension of the Son of God. In case we ever doubted the goodness and sanctity of the human body, there is a man, Jesus Christ, seated at the right hand of God.

The hope of resurrection has its source and surety in the resurrection of Jesus: "We know that Christ, being raised from the dead, will never die again; death no longer has dominion over him" (Rom 6:9). His resurrection is the first fruits of those who have died (1 Cor 15:20). Just as he was raised on the third day, so we will be raised on the last day: "he who raised Jesus from the dead will give life to our mortal bodies" (Rom 8:11). Our bodies are mortal, perishable, corruptible, decaying – an earthly tent (2 Cor 5:1). Resurrection is not the resuscitation of our mortal bodies, the restoration of our earthly tent. When Jesus raised Lazarus from the dead, he was resuscitated. He was not resurrected. Lazarus died again. We still await the fulfillment of Jesus's promise: "I am the resurrection and the life. Whoever believes in me, though he die, yet shall he live" (John 11:25).

The hope of the resurrection is a metamorphosis into glory. When our Saviour returns from heaven, he "will transform our lowly body to be like his glorious body" (Phil 3:21). The Apostle Paul anticipates our question: "But someone will ask, 'How are the dead raised? With what kind of body do they come?'" (1 Cor 15:35). Paul gives us the analogy of the seed and the tree. The mortal body, dead and buried, is like the seed. The resurrected body is like the tree. The analogy gives us a sense of the metamorphosis of the resurrection: "What is sown is perishable; what is raised is imperishable. It is sown in dishonour; it is raised in glory. It is sown in weakness; it is raised in power. It is sown a natural body; it is raised a spiritual body" (1 Cor 15:42-44).

But the analogy can only take us so far: "Behold! I tell you a mystery. We shall not all sleep, but we shall all be changed, in a moment, in the twinkling of an eye, at the last trumpet. For the trumpet will sound, and the dead will be raised imperishable, and we shall be changed" (1 Cor 15:51-52). When Christ returns, we will all be resurrected, whether living or dead. The metamorphosis into glory is a mystery.

Analogy assumes comparison, yet Paul declares, "I consider that the sufferings of this present time are not worth comparing with the glory that is to be revealed to us" (Rom 8:18). The glory to be revealed is the glory of our resurrection. Resurrection is a metamorphosis into an eternal fellowship in glory: "he who raised the Lord Jesus will raise us also with Jesus and bring us with you into his presence" (2 Cor 4:14). God will raise us with Christ and together bring us into his presence.

In this hope of glory, we groan, waiting patiently to be clothed in glory (2 Cor 5:1-4; Rom 8:23). In this hope of glory, we crucify sinful passions and desires: "everyone who thus hopes in him purifies himself as he is pure" (1 John 3:3). In this hope, we labour and serve: "Therefore, my beloved brothers, be steadfast, immovable, always abounding in the work of the Lord, knowing that in the Lord your labour is not in vain" (1 Cor 15:58).

And the Life of the Age to Come

God's Word speaks of two ages, the present evil age and the age to come (Gal 1:3; Mark 10:30). When we are raised on the last day, we will enter the life of the age to come (Luke 20:34-26). Hebrews 11:9-10 reminds us that the saints of old also looked for the age to come: "By faith [Abraham] went to live in the land of promise, as in a foreign land, living in tents with Isaac and Jacob, heirs with him of the same promise. For he was looking forward to the city that has foundations, whose designer and builder is God."

Abraham looked forward to that city, but the Apostle John saw it. He describes his vision in Revelation 21:1-5:

> Then I saw a new heaven and a new earth, for the first heaven and the first earth had passed away, and the sea was no more. And I saw the holy city, new Jerusalem, coming down out of heaven from God, prepared as a bride adorned for her husband. And I heard a loud voice from the throne saying, "Behold, the dwelling place of God is with man. He will dwell with them, and they will be his people, and God himself will be with them as their God. He will wipe away every tear from their eyes, and death shall be no more, neither shall there be mourning, nor crying, nor pain any more, for the former things have passed away."

And again, in Revelation 22:1-5:

> Then the angel showed me the river of the water of life, bright as crystal, flowing from the throne of God and of the Lamb through the middle of the street of the city; also, on either side of the river, the tree of life with its twelve kinds of fruit, yielding its fruit each month. The leaves of the tree were for the healing of the nations. No longer will there be anything accursed, but the throne of God and of the Lamb will be in it, and his servants will worship him. They will see his face, and his name will be on their foreheads. And night will be no more. They will need no light of lamp or sun, for the Lord God will be their light, and they will reign for ever and ever.

The glory of the age to come is the glory of the Triune God, whom we confess in the Nicene Creed. The life of the age to come is life in the eternal light of the Father, Son, and Holy Spirit. Eternal life is life in communion with the Triune God. This is the life Jesus promises: "I give them eternal life, and they will never perish, and no one will snatch them out of my hand" (John 10:28). This life is his own life, which is the very life of God: "For as the Father has life in himself, so he has granted the Son also to have life in himself" (John 5:26).

By faith, we have already received eternal life: "Truly, truly, I say to you, whoever hears my word and believes him who sent me has eternal life" (John 5:24). Even now, we know and have communion with the Triune God: "And this is eternal life, that they know you the only true God, and Jesus Christ whom you have sent" (John 17:3). But, for now, we live in this present evil age and we look for the life of the age to come: "For now we see in a mirror dimly, but then face to face. Now I know in part; then I shall know fully, even as I have been fully known" (1 Cor 13:12).

Coda

I have quoted Gregory of Nazianzus throughout this little book and I want to give him the last word. Gregory reminds us that our confession of faith in the triune God is an expression of our worship: "The sum of the matter is this: worship the Trinity" (*Poem* 1.1.10, 74).[1] The Nicene Creed frames and orients doxology. It places us "within the bounds of reverence" (*Oration* 20.5).[2]

Finally, Gregory reminds us that our worship orients and motivates our witness:

> But when we "guard our soul with all vigilance" (Prov 4:23 LXX) and "build upward paths in the heart" (Ps 83:6 LXX), "breaking up our fallow ground anew" (Jer 4:3) and "sowing the seeds of righteousness" (Hos 10:12), as Solomon and David and Jeremiah advise us to do, and so enkindle within ourselves the light of knowledge – at that

---

1 *On God and Man*, trans. Gilbert, 83.
2 *Gregory of Nazianzus*, trans. Daley, 100–101.

point, let us begin to utter God's wisdom, which is hidden in Mystery, and let us shine forth this light on others. Until then, however, let us first purify ourselves, and be initiated into the Word . . . receiving the Word when he comes – not only receiving him, in fact, but holding on to him and revealing him to others. (*Or.* 39.10)[3]

As we worship and glorify the Father, Son, and Holy Spirit, we cry out with the Psalmist:

> Let the peoples praise you, O God;
> let all the peoples praise you. (Ps 67:3,5)

And let us proclaim the one Lord, Jesus Christ, who for us men and for our salvation, came down from heaven.

---

[3] *Gregory of Nazianzus,* trans. Daley, 132.

www.ingramcontent.com/pod-product-compliance
Lightning Source LLC
Chambersburg PA
CBHW061210070526
44583CB00025B/3197